Bhutan

Künla Khari
7600

Pünsum
7550

N

E

S

Kuru Chu

Pö La

Me La

Mangde Chu

Lhüntse

Dong La

Rodu La

Kurtö

Kora

Bumthang

Bumthang Chu

Kuru Chu

Mt.
20

Mongar

Tashigang

Nyamjang Chu

Mangde Chu

Dangme Chu

Manas Chu

isar

Manas

Darranga

50 km

Heights of mountains in metres

lia

Bhutan

Bhutan

Land of Hidden Treasures

Text by Blanche C. Olschak
Photography by Ursula and Augusto Gansser

Stein and Day, Publishers, New York

First published in the United States of America by Stein and Day, Publishers, 1971
Translated from BHUTAN © Hallwag Verlag, Bern, 1969
This enlarged English version © George Allen & Unwin Ltd, London, and Stein & Day,
New York, 1971
Library of Congress Catalog Card No. 79-137742

Printed in Switzerland
Stein and Day, Publishers, 7 East 48 Street, New York, N. Y. 10017
American ISBN 8128-1357-X

The Mystic Spiral

We entered the temple court of Paro Dzong, the monumental fortress of Western Bhutan. Rows of wooden arches, supported by columns, overhung wall paintings on three sides of the court. We could hardly believe our eyes: the temple door was flanked by frescoes which, step by step, portrayed the radiating evolution of energy into matter. To the left of the eastern gate the fresco of a gigantic mandala shone from the wall. This mandala is surrounded by a 'fire circle' of flaming red. Blue clouds of ether form the background of the circle's inner sphere and at its centre a small triple spiral seems to spin rapidly. It is the symbol of first movement surrounded by large circles floating on the clouds of ether. The circles are painted in fine lines of black and white and in all colours of the rainbow. The latter are symbolic of the four compass directions, red for west, blue for east, yellow for south, and green for north; black stands for the nadir and white for the zenith. The circles intersect and form ellipsoidal lines, emphasising the spherical dimensions. This is a visionary rendering of primary movement: the 'mystic spiral' in the universe, as described in prints that lie forgotten and covered by dust in monastery libraries.

In this mandala, movement was still symbolised by the three-footed spiral, while in later renderings a four-footed swastika was substituted. Around this spiral a whirl circle indicates energies moving in a sphere of future materialisation, in which geometrical figures appear. They are the symbols of the four 'elements', earth, water, fire and air. The yellow square, on the multidimensional level to be realised as a cube, stands for 'earth', the most ancient symbol for solid matter. This cosmic mandala is maintained in the most brilliant colours; it was originally painted by an old Lama, who has long since left the earthly sphere. The deeper meaning of this fresco has become remote and difficult to comprehend even for his successors, but to us it appears strangely real and unbelievably modern.

The Buddhist conception of the universe, based on much older traditions, comprises millions of worlds and astral systems in immeasurable space. It extends over hundreds of millions of years in an endless cycle of evolution, expiration and rebirth. It describes our world as being one diminutive manifestation of countless terrestrial developments of life. Planet Earth, in

5

fact, is called the 'Vessel of All that is Perishable' and is only one in a series of worlds, which together form a thousandfold universe, or chiliocosm, of which again there are many. Each universe in unfathomable space is equilibrated by a 'network' of interwoven cosmic forces. 'Force' and 'energy', indeed, are the words used in the old texts, symbolically termed 'blue-green air', 'wind', 'ether', and depicted by crossed thunderbolts. This is a symbol derived from the archaic weapon in the hands of the old gods, a shaft of lightning preceding a clap of thunder, which in Buddhism became the symbol of spiritual power. Only half a century ago western scientists considered these conceptions merely a mythological phantasm, but to-day we are more aware of the high degree of spiritual reality hidden behind these ancient thought processes. Their colourful renderings on temple walls are intended as provocative 'thinking-tools'. Looking at this 'mystic spiral', we are deeply affected: a spiritual treasure, this cosmic mandala becomes a fascinating recollection of age-old wisdom. It seems like a sign-post to a spiritual bridge which, over an abyss of vanished or vanishing eras, leads to a new epoch in which technical spirals must produce the energies for survival.

The New Airfield and the Old Temple

Paro Dzong, once a mighty fortress, dominates the whole fertile valley of the river Paro Chu. Its round watch-towers, now in ruins, were built on the surrounding ridges at what were once important strategical points. But the biggest, towering above the gigantic square fortress, is now a small national museum. At the foot of the mighty fort, the famous rice fields of the Paro Valley spread out, and rice, of five different kinds, is the country's wealth; thanks to the rain-bringing summer monsoon, it is cultivated to an altitude of 8,500 feet.

Between the rice fields was built the new mountain road that now connects Paro with West Bengal. From the top of the temple tower of Paro Dzong jeeps and cars can be seen driving to a small airfield, the second anniversary of which was celebrated on March 22, 1970. It was a gay festival, held in the traditional fashion, lasting three days; it confirmed the introduction of modern transport into what was once a 'sealed country'. At first sight, this seemed a strange but fascinating development in a terrain which, till very recently, was famous only for an age-old caravan road that led from the 'Roof of the World' to the Indian South.

The technical age made its appearance in Bhutan in an environment filled with most ancient traditions. Facing the new airfield, and nearly hidden in the shadow of the western side of the Paro Valley, stands the country's oldest temple, the Kyichu Lhakhang, and within its courts precious relics of its earliest days, as far back as the beginning of the seventh century, are still preserved. White chörtens—reliquaries—tell of the first Buddhist missionaries who entered Paro from the north at a time when King Songtsängampo ruled on the 'Roof of the World'. This king had taken a vow to spread the Buddhist doctrine, and missionaries wandered in regions stretching from far north of the Silk Road, and embracing the cultural centres of the Tarim Basin, to a long way south-east of the Himalayas. Legend has it that the then mighty Tibetan King had resolved to free the whole of Central Asia and the neighbouring mountain regions from the grip of the heathen demoness, who spread only fear and superstition. To understand this symbolic legend in the light of mythological geography, one has to imagine the outstretched body of the giant demoness lying with her heart at Lhasa, the centre of Tibet, and grasping the borderlands with her claws. A claw of the hind left foot is supposed to have clung threateningly to the site of the present Kyichu Lhakhang, one of the twelve famous temples said to have been founded at that time.

The Visit to the Mountain Goddess

The Paro Chu rises in the north below Chomolhari, the Sovereign Mistress of the Divine Mountain. At the foot of that majestic peak the ruin of a small fortress and the remains of watch-towers can be seen. They stand there, backed only by a no-man's-land of mountain wilderness, dominated by the Divine Mountain. They are relics of an epoch during which, at the beginning of the seventeenth century, Bhutan had to fight for its independence; but the jagged walls of snow and ice of the unconquerable glacier frontier rise inaccessible above them. Even for these 'Thrones of the Gods' a new era has begun, however genuinely graced by Bhutanese participation, for in April 1970 a joint Indo-Bhutanese expedition paid its respects to the mountain goddess. The event must be recorded in the words of the young Bhutanese Second-Lieutenant Chachu, for they are characteristic of the sudden clash between old and modern times, between a technical-material and a religious-spiritual culture. It might sound strange, but these Bhutanese, given the right chance and the proper moment, would have the inherent ability to combine them!

'For our people the 24,000 feet Chomolhari is a very holy mountain, since it is the abode of the Goddess *Jo-mo lHa-ri*. Most of the Bhutanese believe that the sacred peaks cannot be climbed. Such feelings are prevalent among all hill people. It is probably because mountains play such an important part in our lives. I, too, was brought up in such an atmosphere and always thought that Chomolhari was a sacred mountain, never to be trodden by men.'

Nevertheless, it was a pleasant surprise for Lt. Chahu to be given the privilege of joining the summit party of the Indo-Bhutanese expedition sponsored by the King of Bhutan, who—always combining modern efforts with old traditions—had provided a brass image of Lord Buddha, duly sanctified by the blessings of the Lamas, to be placed on the summit along with the flags of Bhutan and India.

'We were moving together as a team, like a family moving to Chomolhari on a pilgrimage. The base camp was established on April 14th, at an altitude of 16,500 feet, just below the ice. The great sacred peak of Chomolhari could be seen, looming above us, calling to us with all its majesty. It was an awe-inspiring sight. A party of three managed to find a route up to 19,000 feet and Camp I was established there on April 18th.'

Three days later Camp II was pitched at 23,000 feet, and on April 23rd, at 4.30 a. m., Lt. Chachu started out with his team of five:

'It was a clear day. I prayed for a while and then we all started moving up. Dangerous stretches had to be traversed over which we belayed each other. Steps had to be kicked or cut into snow and ice.'

They reached the south-western summit after some hours and, having rested a while, proceeded towards the main summit:

8

'After what appeared to be days we were near the summit, about a hundred feet below it. I looked up towards the seat of the Goddess Chomolhari and something happened to me. I felt that I would not go up to the top. I was too steeped in the traditions of my country to break with them so suddenly. I decided that I would stay where I was and it was with much reluctance and after great argument that the other members left me there after securing and anchoring me safely. They said there was nothing wrong with going to the abode of the Goddess Chomolhari to pray. We all had come there in utter humility on a pilgrimage. That is the way of mountaineers: they love and respect the mountains and do not climb them to desecrate them. A little later, the four members returned after planting our flags on the summit. They also left a holy urn with the image of Buddha, blessed by the holy Lamas, in the snow on the summit.'

They returned to Camp II, where they met the second summit party, who proceeded in high spirits to achieve their goal. But theirs was an unlucky attempt. An abrupt change of weather occurred, the second party was lost and could not be traced despite the closest search.

'It was with heavy hearts', Lt. Chachu says, 'that the search was finally abandoned. . . . It all looked rather tiring while it lasted, but given a chance now I would again like to go to the mountains. They are so good. You feel their sacredness. Mountains do something to men. Once you have been to them you are never the same again. Once you have been on a mountain you feel yourself a purer, a better man.'

The Tiger's Den

Wherever one wanders in the mountain wilderness, to the farthest inhabited places and the highest mountain passes, the signs of holy places are the religious monuments and symbols, the mani-stones, chörten-reliquaries and prayer-flags. The mystic formula OM MANI PADME HUM are cut into stone and rocks and into the slabs of prayer-walls. This holy formula cannot be translated literally; its deeper meaning is felt by all, that the divine power—inborn every human being, but covered with the dust of ignorance—might become manifest within us. This Mani-formula, derived from the 'Script of Gods', is cast or embossed in the copper mantles of the prayer-wheels of all sizes. The big wheels are hidden within square shrines, erected above rivulets, and are revolved by water power to multiply the blessings. And countless prayer-flags, of every size and colour, wave above all holy places, spreading the Buddhist wish for luck and happiness for all beings, so carrying it in the wind in all directions. Attached to bamboo flag-poles, erected in lines, these prayer-flags show the way to the temples and monasteries that are the pilgrim's goal.

From Dukgyäl Dzong, with great round watch-towers that once protected the western side of Paro Valley, the view opens to Chomolhari, a white and shining pyramid, indeed a majestic throne for the Mountain Goddess. Small paths lead through the highland jungles to the Hädi Gömpa, a solitary monastery hidden in the mist and snow. Only occasionally is a lonely pilgrim to be found, murmuring prayers and turning his prayer-wheel, within which is a small thin script-roll, printed with blessings and holy formulas; it rotates and is supposed to promulgate a thousand times the good wishes dedicated to the benefit of all beings. In winter ice-crystals sparkle and glitter on the moss veils that hang from the branches of the trees.

We were two days on the road that passed through dense forests from Dukgyäl Dzong by way of Hädi Gömpa, when suddenly we came upon a magnificent view from a precipice, that was like a picture framed in these mossy veils. High up in the rocks, built on the sheer face of the cliff, we saw Taktshang, the Tiger's Den, a monastery founded at the end of the eighth century. Tigers, which have now found their last retreat in the southern jungles, once roamed here in the mountains, and men were terrified both by them and by demons. So pious Buddhist hermits purified the region and tamed the demons, and their retreats, now deserted, are still to be seen. They cling to the rock walls like nests, built near springs, and can only be reached by step-ladders, like the small hermitage on the precipice below the Tiger's Den.

In summer, when the rain-bringing south wind blows against the Himalayan chain, the Tiger's Den seems to float avove the clouds. It is now a whole complex of buildings, chapels and temples, erected in the nail-less frame-work style and repaired every year; but it is only accessible by a   10 single steep path. On top of the ridge opposite, the new chief monastery has been built. When we visited it, the monks were busy printing large new prayer-flags; with their wooden printing-blocks and the cotton material to print upon, they sat on the balconies of the monastery roof, urged along in their work by the desire to produce more prayer-flags for the next religious ceremony, so to spread more Buddhist blessings in the wind.

Hero and Mask Dances in Paro

From the new chief monastery of Tiger's Den a broad and easy road leads down to the valley, along to Paro Dzong which, according to old tradition, embraces the secular as well as the religious centres of the district. On New Year's Day, which, according to the moon-calendar is at the beginning or end of February, and is one of the biggest religious festivals, the whole of Paro Dzong becomes alive. An enormous thanka, the greatest treasure of the Paro Monastery, is hung out over the wall of the temple court. It is a picture-scroll, an old appliqué-work made by monks, stitching pieces of silk together and embroidering the whole with golden thread. It depicts Guru Rimpoché flanked by two Mystic Consorts. He is the 'Lotus-born', Padmasambhava-Pämajungnä, the great missionary and miracle-worker who, at the end of the eighth century, tamed the heathen demons and converted them to Buddhism. Usually called Guru Rimpoché, i. e. 'Precious Teacher', by the adherents of the old sect, the Nyingmapa, he is venerated like a second Buddha.

Before this thanka the dramatic spectacle of the religious mask-pageants is given a lengthy performance. At the beginning, and between the ritual dances, the Hero Dance takes place. The dancers appear in dark blue, widely pleated long robes, girt with sword-belts. Their heads are crowned by the 'Rings of Knighthood'. Some of them wear helmets and wield buckler-shields covered with rhino skin. Very solemnly they perform their knightly dances. With Thunderbolt-Steps they symbolically trample all evil underfoot, and by thrusts of their swords cut through the clouds of ignorance. Their ceremonial round-dance is followed by the masked dancers, who all wear short skirts of silk of every colour. Out from the curtains of the temple door they leap into the court, every step stimulated by the thunderous rhythm of the monks' orchestra, which, with drums beating and trumpets sounding, is hidden in a balcony overhanging the temple court. Every movement of the dancers has its symbolic meaning. During the dances with the small and the big drums all malevolent demons are chased away by the rolling sounds. The Stag Dancers, with their nodding antlered masks, decorated with flapping wings, represent the archaic idea of cannibal demons of forgotten ages. But they, too, are converted, taking a vow to help protect religion and giving the promise to return the next year. The Cemetery Dancers, with their wrathful death-masks, remind everyone that all life is perishable and that the search for worldly pleasure is illusory. But this is not by any means regarded as a sinister spectacle; on the contrary, it is looked upon as an important stimulus to accumulating good deeds in this life, thereby guaranteeing a good life to follow, or—as it is popularly said—rebirth in paradise.

These religious and mask-dances, as well as tournaments, are very popular Bhutanese festivals; everyone takes part. The children of the primary school, where English is now taught, watch with the same enthusiasm as the great ministers and the members of the National Assembly. Their mothers are with them, lovingly carrying their babies on their backs. Thus the youngest members of the family, safely secured by straps of woven material to the backs of elder relatives, enjoy—with their heads at the same height as the adults—all the thrilling spectacles and never cry. All the spectators, watching and singing and laughing, crowd together around the stage-court, and the dancing acts can continue for several days, during which the men may participate in archery competitions. Jesters, wearing burlesque masks, attack the watchers with provocative humour and never tire of performing their endles pranks, and raise wild laughter with their witticisms. No person is safe from their ridicule; buffoonery knows no limits and is universally refreshing. After the festival the weapons, masks and old costumes are stored away, and the most precious of them are hung on the walls of the closed temple of the Protective Deities.

Ritual and lay dances are the most cherished folk-art of Bhutan. They are performed by men, who display all their grace and rhythmic strength. They train in this style of dancing throughout the year. The women have

12

their special share, filling in the intervals in a most dignified way, with a kind of standing round-dance, marking time with small steps. They have beautiful voices and they sing the old songs of the mountain people, handed down from mythological times. But if Bhutanese women hold this position in dance-dramas, it should not be mistaken as a matter of 'background'. On the contrary, the Bhutanese, like all Bhutian and Tibeto-Burmese women, have always held a prominent position in society, with at least equal rights, voting and ruling included. Therefore, they have had no reason to dance attendance on men, but only to applaud the display of their hero's prowess. This feature of Bhutanese life was already emphasised by the earliest explorers, like Samuel Turner, who visited Western Bhutan in 1800.

Nail-less Architecture and Wheel-less Traffic

On the new road which connects Paro with Thimphu, the capital, progress is evident. Here the old fortress, religious and administrative centre of the Thimphu district, as well as of the whole country, is built on the banks of the Wang Chu. But the old dzong became too small for all the new offices now necessary for the 'development wing' and the attached ministries; so the King in 1965 ordered new buildings to be built, which was done simultaneously with the new road. That, too, was a highly appreciated, symbolic arrangement, giving space not only for new roads but also for new life in the old dzong. The new wings, attached to the old constructions, were erected in the traditional style of nail-less framework. This rebuilding of the Thimphu Dzong is a striking example of how old customs need not be forgotten in a new epoch, which has begun to furnish the houses of the capital with electricity, heating and telephones: a rather unbelievable thought for all those who only yesterday visited Thimphu, situated at a height of 8,500 feet.

Not only was Bhutanese architecture nail-less; Bhutanese labour and traffic was 'wheel-less'; no wheeled trek-wagons of any kind were used. Elderly people and dignitaries, on special occasions, were carried in palanquins, borne on the shoulders of men. The wheel-lessness of

13

Bhutanese Himalayan and Tibetan cultures was everywhere stressed, and was evident from the beginning of documented history. But to the surprise of all, something 'unique' was found among the labourers on the buildings: a two-wheeled, simple dray-cart for the heavy stone loads, which had always been used by the Bhutia-Tibetan tribes. Attention had already been drawn to this wooden two-wheeled cart, overlooked by most travellers, by F. Spencer Chapman as the only wheeled vehicle in Lhasa. Women were used to draw it for the transport of stone blocks in building the foundation-walls of the houses, exactly as they were used, in the same traditional way, for the new dzong buildings in Thimphu.

Monasteries and fortifications are built on the hill-tops surrounding the Thimphu Valley. These buildings are monuments of Bhutanese history, reminiscent of Zhabdung I, the founder of the then theocratic Kingdom of Bhutan. In the north, high above Thimphu, the 'Iron-Mountain Monastery' is hidden in the mountain jungles. It was erected in memory of Zhabdung I, who entered this place around 1600. In the great temple hall of this Cäri Gömpa are shown the horns of the yak which he rode. A series of beautiful painted scrolls hang on the pillars. They depict the spiritual line of the incarnations of the Zhabdungs who reigned up to the nineteenth century.

Archery Competition in Thimphu

In the Middle Ages the Bhutanese were renowned warriors, and were said to be the best archers in the Himalayan region. Archery is still a favourite folk-sport. An archery competition in the Thimphu Valley, which we were able to witness, gave us the best insight into the life of these people, who still know how to celebrate their national festivals with unparalleled abandon. There is an enormous gaiety, mirrored in the colourful patterns of the national dresses. The inhabitants of two small neighbouring villages had met for the competition. One small tent was set up for the bows and the arrows, skilfully made of bamboo, the quivers, hanging left and right of the entrance to the 'weapon tent', were masterpieces of bamboo work.

A long bamboo section was used for them, carefully over-plaited with multi-coloured patterns of bamboo bast. There were 'folding-bows' also, for transport and travelling, which can be folded up. A second, bigger tent was erected for tea. Gay crowds encircled the shooting-grounds. The target, set up at a distance of several hundred feet, was a very small circle. The men strutted along, proudly displaying the national costume, which consists of a long coat, woven in stripes, cut similar to a kimono. It is lifted up to the waist, draped in folds at the back and held together by a slim hand-woven waistband. At the front, the dress forms a large 'breast-pocket' in which the Bhutanese men carry everything necessary, not only loose paper-money and lunch baskets, but even needles and coins, which they produce in no time. Sometimes the contents of this breast-pocket, filling the upper part of the dress, suggest a false corpulence. A small straight sword is worn at the girdle by all men, a useful instrument with which, if necessary, even a bamboo hut can be built very quickly. Even the earliest travellers to Bhutan were amazed to see that every Bhutanese, included the servants, bore a sword and that all of them wore the same dress, only the patterns changing according to personal taste. To some these seemed insignificant folk-habits; nevertheless—as George Brogle observed 200 years ago—they must be regarded as the signs of a basic and potentially democratic society in which king and servants wear the same clothes. These Bhutian habits have survived practically from the nation's earliest days, and they may well provide the strength to make the right sort of contact with those innovations which are absolutely necessary for survival to-day, without losing the traditional background.

But there were no such discussions at the archery competition. The games began. With shining eyes, they sighted the target, carefully fixed the arrow, and seldom missed the mark. When an arrow hit the centre of the target, the marksman jubilantly leapt into the air. The Bhutanese participate in these competitions passionately, almost with inborn enthusiasm, but—very important—a loser is never angry. If they sing, they sing with devotion; and if they dance, they just throw every possible kind of physical and emotional expression into their movements. They understand quite well how to combine three kinds of aboriginal folk-art—singing, dancing and shooting—and they never miss any opportunity to display their talent.

During the intervals of an archery competition tea and 'chang' are consumed, without getting drunk. The women form a ring, executing a standing round dance, and begin singing. Their dresses follow the finest folk-tradition, each being a hand-woven masterpiece: every valley has its own colourful pattern, the flower-ornaments of the East being especially esteemed. Every woman's dress, the most precious being woven of Bhutanese silk in double-sided patterns, has a secret. It is neither cut nor sewn. Worn over a silk long-sleeved blouse, it consists of a 'sheet' of three woven strips, each strip being an elbow-length wide and four ells long, an old ell being about $21^{1}/_{2}$ inches. This beautifully woven 'sheet' has to be most carefully pleated and draped around the body. At the shoulders it is held together by silver buckles, which are connected by a chain ornamented with lucky golden symbols. These buckles replace the old-time fibulas, which are now rarely seen, all being collector's pieces. The long dress is held together around the waist with a long woven sash of matching colours and at least a foot wide. The women wear necklaces of coral and turquoise strung together with silver amulets. The most precious pieces are the oval beads, or 'tears of the Gods'; they are so-called 'eye-stones', consisting of some strangely treated agates with dark-brown tiger-stripes and 'eye-rings', nine of them being auspicious. Their pattern decides their value. They are family treasures and highly cherished by all Bhutias. They once were found in old graves, said to belong to the epic period of Gesar, the great hero of the Central Asian saga. A Bhutanese festival, indeed, is a live display of folk-art and tradition, and helps us to understand these mountain people.

National dress is obligatory for all Bhutanese, with the exception of footwear. But on festival occasions one still sees the beautiful traditional boots. The soles are of soft leather, the leg is appliqué-work, made of colourful pieces of felt for winter boots, and cotton for summer. The legs of the men's pantaloons are stuffed into the boot-legs and fine woven boot-straps, often of silk, and in days gone by woven between two gazelle horns, are used to hold the boot-legs in place. The male costume is embellished, furthermore, by a kind of cotton or silk vest, with a collar and broad, white, shining cuffs at the sleeve ends.

16

The Glacier of the Three Spiritual Brothers

From Thimphu the road to Punakha leads eastwards over the Dochu La. From this pass the view opens upon the magnificent panorama of the glacier-covered chain that forms Bhutan's northern frontier. These 'Thrones of the Gods' are most impressive. Next to Chomolhari in the west is Tsering Kang, the 'Glacier of Long Life', followed by Masa Kang, once venerated as the divine mountain-ancestor of the Masang, a powerful tribe which is said to have ruled in prehistoric times. Masang was, too, the ancestor of Gesar, the unconquerable 'Great Lion', the hero of every Bhutia. It was predicted that he would be reborn if ever his people were in great danger. The lovely songs of the Gesar epic were once sung all over the 'Roof of the World'; now they are still to be heard among the Bhutanese, who enrich the festivals, as well as their every-day life, with these beautiful melodies.

In the centre of this chain of mountains towers Kangkar Pünsum, the 'White Glacier of the Three Spiritual Brothers', a name which symbolises the once peaceful co-existence of three peoples, the Bhutanese, the aboriginal Mön-pa and the Tibetans of the north. But Kangkar Pünsum, with all the other mountains gods, now watches over a frontier which to-day is hermetically sealed. It has a few so-called 'one man passes' at a height of over 15,000 feet, but only the two 'easy passes', in the extreme west and extreme east of the country, were ever a practical link between the peoples, then on friendly terms, who exchanged their goods in the bazaars at the foot of the south-eastern Himalayas.

At the far eastern end of the glacier panorama towers another mountain giant, popularly named Zhugthi Kang, the 'Throne of the Gods' of Kurtö district. Below that glacier wall the small 'Lion Fortress' was built; its classical name Sengge Dzong is spelled Singyi Dzong in eastern Bhutanese. The district centre of Kurtö is Lhüntse Dzong, situated on the northern mountain track connecting the district of Kurtö with Tashiyangtse in the east.

Besides the mountains of the north, all the northern part of the country can be seen from Dochu La. Mountain ridges shelter the inhabited fertile valleys, which are separated, as well as connected, by high mountain passes. The highest situated settlement in Bhutan prospers at an altitude of 12,300 feet: this is Thanza, in the remote Lunana, which was colonized by the people of Punakha. It can be reached only by difficult passes, snow-bound in winter. The people of Laya, whose settlements are shielded in the high north by the Masa Kang, live at a height of 11,400 feet; they speak a dialect of the old-Tibetan tongue. The women of Laya wear clothes that are woven from oily sheep's wool, with beautiful patterns. They wear their hair down to the shoulders, and their heads are crowned by small pointed bamboo hats, which look very strange in an environment of snow and ice. North of Laya and Lunana there is nothing but mountain wilderness. The small forts of Lingzhi and Gaza are situated south of Laya. They were of great importance for the growing power and stability of Bhutan.

Forts and Iron-chain Bridges

Bhutan has the longest and most beautiful chain of still unconquered Himalayan peaks. From Dochu La the road leads to Punakha Dzong, a fortress built at the confluence of the 'Father and Mother Rivers', Mo Chu and Pho Chu, a point also called the 'Marriage of the Rivers'. Swinging suspension-bridges once connected the banks with the Dzong. Originally they were made of iron chain. We saw one of these constructions, but made of iron-cables according to the old style, with bamboo cross-pieces to walk on and bamboo wattles to protect the sides. All the old constructions have been washed away by the torrents that rush down from the melting snows during the monsoon, but iron-chain suspension-bridges were once the characteristic crossings of the broad and powerful mountain rivers. They were constructed in the fifteenth century by the famous iron-bridge builder, Thangthong Gyalpo, who worked in Central Asia as well as in the Himalayas; his most famous bridge spans the Kyichu river, south of Lhasa. From a modern point of view he was the pioneer engineer of Central Asia; but with the development of a religious culture which put greater emphasis on spiritual values than on technical progress, he has been venerated merely as a saint and miracle-worker and is said to have created his works by supernatural powers. His family monastery and retreat is situated in Bhutan, 18 between Paro and Thimphu; it crouches against red ferruginous rocks, which were once an open iron working but are no longer profitable. One of his big bridge chains is still kept in the monastery as a precious relic. Thangthong Gyalpo was famous also as an architect. His 'Cylinder Temple' is situated on the western bank of the Paro Valley, just opposite the Kyichu Lhakhang. Statues, created by Thangthong Gyalpo, still grace the temple, and reputedly self-created speaking images are hidden in the altar niches. But only a few old people know about Thangthong Gyalpo and his once famous creations. Soon new bridges will be constructed in Punakha. At the junction of Father and Mother rivers, just in front of Punakha Dzong, stands a very small fort with round towers, to-day a temple. It is watched over by an old monk, who cultivates his gardens on the hill-sides below the strong walls and he proudly shows his big citrus fruits, which grow here even in the winter. From Punakha Dzong the way east leads to another imposing fort: Wangdiphodang Dzong. Zhabdung I is named as its founder. In a creative vision, it is said, he saw the fortifications he wanted erected and he knew how to inspire his architects. Once, on the confluence of the two rivers that embrace the present Wangdiphodang Dzong, he saw a little boy playing in the sand and erecting a dzong of pebbles. This was taken as a good omen, and exactly at this point Zhabdung I ordered the building of the new dzong, which was named after the boy who was called Wangdi.

Enchanting Guest-Dancers in Tongsa

From Wangdiphodang the way continues east, over bamboo suspension bridges and narrow mountain paths. Steep rock steps must be climbed up and down; the horses are dismounted and carefully led. From these rock stairways the first view of Tongsa Dzong, the 'Fort above the New Village', is obtained. But it takes hours more to reach it along the serpentine path that winds around the hillside. Tongsa Dzong is the ancestral residence of the Bhutanese royal family, the Lords of Tongsa. The western part of the building, founded by Zhabdung I, was later enlarged and now embraces twenty temples, which can be recognized from far away by the small golden symbols that crown the roofs above the altar.

In Tongsa Dzong many ancient customs are preserved, including a special way of welcoming important guests. From the strong western walls the caravan of approaching visitors can be observed until it slowly approaches up the last rock steps. As soon as the head of the column of horses reaches the small chapel at the cross-way which leads straight up to the steps of the dzong, the trumpets sound. Monks, standing on the walls, beating drums and blowing horns, give the first welcome, and soon a unique spectacle begins. The moment the caravan has reached the first steps leading to the fortress, the lay-dancers of Tongsa Dzong swarm out to 'dance' the visitors in and conduct them to the guest house. This ancient custom symbolises the clearing of all evil from the guests' path, trampling under foot, with 'thunderbolt steps', all the demons which might possibly disturb genuine hospitality. The dancers are all men and well trained in this most popular Bhutanese folk-art throughout the year. On this occasion they do not wear masks; they wear the usual short dancing-skirts, made of pieces of gaily coloured silk, which swing rhythmically with their movements. Their heads are graced by beautiful headgear with nodding ornaments and flapping lappets. The costumes, which have such a bewildering effect, are part of the treasure of Tongsa Dzong and are only worn on special occasions. The dancing is supplemented by the smoke of fragrant twigs, which are burnt to cleanse the air of all evil. The guests are led by the dancers in a colourful procession; they cross the many courts of the dzong and are finally led out of the fort to the guest-house, built at the foot of the neighbouring hillside. The path is decorated with yellow flowers, tagetes, the only ones that bloom during the Himalayan winter.

Looking out of the guest-house windows, the row of dancers looks like something from a fairy tale of an enchanted world. Around can be seen houses on which thread-crosses are mounted, a custom reminiscent of Shamanist times long past. The basic form of a thread-cross is made by two sticks which are bound together to form a cross; the ends of the sticks are connected with coloured thread so that it assumes finally a shape similar to a cob-web. These thread-crosses are supposed to be 'demon-traps', catching evil doers before they can enter a house.

The many courts of Tongsa Dzong abound in beautiful frame-work galleries connecting the different buildings. There is quite a spectacle when the

Big Bell sounds, because it calls the monks together; in their swinging dark-red robes, they rush across to the main court, and it is an unforgettable picture to see the great mass celebrated in the main temple. The Lamas sit to the right and left of the way to the altar. Every monk's seat is flanked by a standing drum, which is beaten by a crooked metal instrument. An arched window looks out over the court.

Suddenly a shrill neighing of the 'King's horse' is heard; through the wide open gate it enters the fortress at full gallop, returning from its grand tour of the district. This, too, is a very ancient ceremony that is still maintained. The white, highly bred horse is dismounted, but majestically decorated with the full royal harness and insignia. It wears a golden headdress with a white yak-tail. Ribbons of rainbow hues, attached to its harness, flutter around the horse. This is the ceremony of the 'King's wandering horse', which we were lucky enough to witness in Tongsa Dzong.

Gourmets in the Upland Jungles

In Tongsa Dzong we had to change horses, saddles and grooms. According to custom it is the pride, as well as duty and business, of every district to provide a traveller with accommodation. So it happened that we finally sat on archaic wooden saddles, each worthy of a place in a museum. They were decorated with distinguished saddle-cloths and carpets, and they had big round stirrups of bronze, embossed with symbols. But the mounts, white and grey, were luck-bringing horses. Each knew its way and carried us safely along the edges of precipices and through dense forests, in which—around Tongsa—monkeys chattered in loud protest against the invaders of the high jungles.

Beyond Tongsa Dzong, the real 'Wild East' of Bhutan begins: regions which are still partly unknown and filled with unexplored treasures of folk-art and history. There we began to discover Bhutan as a 'Land of Hidden Treasures'. But slowly we became conscious of the deeper meaning of the name. So it was good to proceed without haste, in the old-fashioned way, and to accommodate ourselves step by step, and day by day, to an environment so fascinating and strange. Only in this way could we absorb the small details that are so very important to filling out the picture of everyday Bhutanese life.

The path led over passes again, passes crowned by mani-stones and prayer-flags, and through dense forests with an abundance of northern as well as southern vegetation. Everything seemed to grow there: conifers of every species, together with rhododendrons and bamboos, and orchids clinging to the gigantic trees. Near villages and temples the holy formula *Om Mani Padme Hum* was everywhere, cut into stones and spreading its peaceful message in all directions. The villages were few, with fertile fields between. The shingle roofs of the houses were covered with stones as protection against storm and wind. Red chillis were spread out between the stones on the roofs, drying in the sun. The farmer's wife cooked the finest home-made noodles on a hearth, which was an oven without chimney or flue. An unsuspecting traveller might mistake them as imported, if not initiated into the culinary secrets of these mountain people. Some of them sat around cross-legged, sewing their boots, which were the most practical footwear for the region. Other villagers were skilled in bamboo plaiting and in manufacturing draught screens, baskets, hats and even bamboo roofs for granaries.

The houses have glassless arched windows, which may be closed from inside by wooden shutters. There is no stove or fireplace to warm the rooms. The only traditional means of heating, which seems to have been inherited from Central Asian tent-dwellers, is not really a brazier, but a big open fire-bowl of bronze or iron. It is placed in the centre of the room, and everyone warms his fingers at the glowing wood. It is a beautiful open fire if the wood is dry, but smoke accumulates if the twigs are wet, and this can only escape through the windows. Sometimes a bonfire is kindled on an open meadow, protected only by bamboo wind-shields. But the national meal, a kind of meat-curry with chilli, is all one can wish for, provided one's taste is fairly exotic. The large round 'red rice' and the long white 'royal rice' provide the basic nourishment. There is also *thugpa,* meat soup, which opens the morning and midday meals; it abounds in the fresh and fragrant herbs of the south-eastern Himalayas. Herbs, spices and medicinal plants have always been a Bhutanese export. And the foreign traveller is reminded that, some 2,000 years ago, rice, noodles, curries,

22

spices and, of course, silk materials were introduced into Europe over the famous Silk Road which connected Central Asia with Asia Minor and southern Europe.

Dried yak-meat is produced, very like the air-dried beef, sliced paper thin, of the Swiss canton of Grisons. 'Meat powder', made from very dry yakmeat, is kept in leather bags and is the most practical instant bouillon for travellers. Milk powder is also manufactured, the milk being dried on skins. Dried cheese, in small cubes, is put on strings and worn by pilgrims like a necklace; in spiced soup it tastes delicious. Butter is preserved with salt. The famous butter-tea has an unjustifiably bad reputation among foreign travellers: it should be sipped, not as 'tea', but as a very strong tea-bouillon, made from green tea-leaves and beaten up with butter and salt. It is an interesting fact that, according to recent tests, tea is the proper drink to balance the undesirable effects of a too fatty diet; so, butter-tea seems to be the right thing for high mountain regions. Making butter-tea is quite a ceremony for the Bhutanese, accompanied by lovely melodies handed down from ancient times. Among this gay and happy people, it is wonderful to hear the Himalayan highlanders' songs accompanying every activity, work, play or festival, and also the preparation of tea. The famous 'tea song' belongs to the Gesar Epic, which celebrates Gesar, the Masang Scion, whose ancestor-mountain—as mentioned before—watches over the north-western frontier of Bhutan. This tea song is really a poetic recipe:

> *Lu alä thalä thalä re*
> Tea leaves have to be used as tenderly as by Gesar's wife!
> *Lu alä thalä thalä re*
> Salt has to be added as sparingly as by a cautious man!
> *Lu alä thalä thalä re*
> Butter has to be added as richly as by a hungry man!
> *Lu alä thalä thalä re*
> Tea has to be beaten as strongly as by a furious man!
> *Lu alä thalä thalä re*
> Tea should be served as politely as by a modest man!
> *Lu alä thalä thalä re*
> Tea should be sipped at royal ease as by King Gesar himself!
> *Lu alä thalä thalä re*

23

On special occasions butter-tea is served with sweet rice that has been cooked with milk and sugar, and mixed with raisins and butter, a complete meal in itself. Puffed rice is much liked too; it is roasted on glowing iron plates and served in round, double, bamboo baskets, so carefully plaited that they survive any expedition. But the Himalayan highlanders have also their secret mountain recipes, strong food intended to prevent mountain sickness and to help resist the cold. Before leaving on a difficult tour over high passes the host himself serves the morning soup. But on this occasion *chang* is added, a spirit distilled from cereals. It is commonly served from a bamboo bottle, made from a single closed bamboo section, provided with a hole and a stopper. This natural bottle is covered with multi-coloured bamboo plaiting and slung from the shoulders on a leather strap.

This description of Himalayan food and drink would not be complete without mentioning the staple food of roasted wheat flour, which is replaced by rice in the lower regions of Bhutan, 'lower' meaning below 9,000 feet. Specially prepared for use against sickness and headache at altitudes over 12,000 feet, the roasted wheat flour is mixed with sugar, tea and *chang* and formed into small balls which taste like marzipan.

We had experience also of their open-air cooking. Nothing is more beautiful than a camp on a meadow in the hills. Instead of tents, small huts, quickly constructed of bamboo screens, are set up. The kitchen is an open fire-place, protected only by bamboo wind-screens. At first, as always on tour, water is boiled in a big kettle for washing after a whole day on horse-back. More water is then used for tea, if desired, without butter for foreigners. In the meantime, the cook, who always accompanies old-fashioned expeditions on horseback, begins his auspicious work. There is no need to carry food in these fertile regions; even in winter there are vegetables and herbs to enrich egg, pork and chicken meals, served with mountains of rice. There is also a kind of luck-bringing pastry, so carefully made that its true place is a handicraft exhibition. The pastry is rolled into beautiful flat shapes and symbols, both round and square, and they follow meander and swastika patterns; nor is the spiral missing.

The 'farewell tea' ceremony is still occasionally performed. Among friends it was once customary to accompany the parting guest to the site of his first midday rest. Quite naturally, a 'party' was planned, and some persons hurried ahead to arrange the resting-place, which was decorated with flowers and marked out by freshly cut twigs. Saddle-rugs were spread on the ground to ensure a comfortable seat; the fire was lit and the tea was ready the moment the guests appeared. Before the final parting there was a long exchange of *khadags,* white scarves which grace all ceremonies of welcome or farewell, and are offered like bouquets or garlands in other countries.

The Castle of the White Bird

With every pass we crossed we moved further east. Mani-stones, as everywhere, graced those passes. The holy formula *Om Mani Padme Hum* was carved upon the piled stones, and new uncarved stones had been added by most pilgrims. Above the mani-stones the usual prayer-flags, attached to bamboo poles, stirred in the wind. Finally we reached our main goal; the path opened upon a ridge from which we could overlook the whole valley of Bumthang, where, at an altitude of 8,500 feet, cranes remain during the winter. They circled over Bjakar Dzong, the 'Castle of the White Bird', whose shining white walls grow out of the hill-side and dominate the largest highland plain of Bhutan. On the western side of the fort, rising above all the other buildings, is the old round tower. It is said that originally a small fort was erected at the eastern end of Bumthang at a position which was strategically unsatisfactory. So all knights, lamas and astrologers assembled to find a better place for a new stronghold. There they sat discussing the problem, but without finding a solution, until suddenly a big white bird, surely the King of the Geese, rose into the air and, crossing the highland plain, settled down on a hill-spur on its eastern side. This was taken as an omen, and the new dzong, which was called 'Castle of the White Bird', was built there.

The Story of King Sindhu Râja of Bumthang

At the end of the eighth century, a long time before the Castle of the White
Bird was erected, a mighty king ruled in Bumthang. He was called Sindhu
Râja, as he was an immigrant from India (a name derived from the river
Indus, originally written Sindhu). The vanishing ruins of his Iron Castle
on the Camkhar Chu, north-west of Bjakar Dzong, are still to be seen. In
an old print, describing the hidden treasures of Bumthang, the Iron Castle
is mentioned as having held all the world's treasures. But the prosperous
years did not last long; Sindhu Râja had an enemy in the south, a king
known as 'Big Nose', who attacked the frontier of Bumthang. So the country
had to be armed at all points, and at a great ceremony all the local guardian
deities were invoked to join together to produce victory. But in vain; in the
very first battle the Crown Prince of Bumthang was killed. Sindhu Râja
was so desperate that he gave up all belief in the help of the gods and
ordered that all temples be desecrated and destroyed. The deities, deeply
offended by having been made responsible for human error, grew angry and
decided to teach Sindhu Râja a lesson. Misfortune befell the whole country.
The King fell very ill; greatly wasted, he lay dying, and people whispered
that the angry gods had taken away his 'vital strength' and that his 'breath
of life' was fading. Everybody felt unhappy and helpless.

Finally, the astrologers and the knights from every remote corner of the
country hurried to the Iron Castle to discuss what could be done to save
the people and the King. Help was urgently needed, because the enemy was
again approaching. But whatever the astrologers suggested, nothing seemed
able to change the evil destiny of the kingdom. Finally, one of them
remembered Guru Rimpoché, the great converter and miracle worker of
Uddyâna, who happened to be in Tibet, taming the heathen demons there.
So they sent him a message, together with cups filled with gold-dust as a
gift, inviting the famous Guru to come and help. He accepted and with his
retinue came to the south-eastern Himalayas, then known as the 'Land of
Mön'. But even for him, the unconquerable converter of all demons, it was
difficult to pacify the angry deities of Bumthang, who had been so deeply
offended by the King. Guru Rimpoché had to use all his magic power to
conquer the local deities. To attract them, he arranged the first festival of

26

ritual dances in Bumthang, and for this he transformed himself into eight manifestations and displayed the eight forms of dance necessary to destroy evil powers. It was an incredible spectacle.

Exactly as he wished, even the head of the local deities approached in haste, not wanting to miss the great drama; but he manifested himself in the shape of a lion. Guru Rimpoché immediately realized the danger and knew that the lion-demon had stolen the King's 'vital strength'. Guru Rimpoché therefore transformed himself into the primeval bird Garuda, spread his eagle-wings and swooped down on the demon, fastening his talons into the lion's neck. A great fight ensued, which ended when Guru Rimpoché succeeded in wresting the King's 'vital factor' from the lion's claws.

Thus Sindhu Râja and his people were saved. Thankfully they took an oath to follow Buddhism and to reestablish all the holy places. The performance of Guru Rimpoché's magic dances constituted the introduction of ritual dancing in Bumthang. The legend is told in many versions; it has an interesting kernel of historical truth, but the bards do not tire of adding oral traditions, herein briefly told. They embellish it with shamanistic details of magic transformations and enchantments characteristic of pre-Buddhist times.

The old print in which the life-story of Sindhu Râja is described is one of the hidden book treasures of Bumthang. It is recorded there that Guru Rimpoché finally succeeded in bringing about a lasting peace between the two warring kings. It is also recorded that the 'Temple of the Future Buddha', the Jampa Lhakhang, already one hundred years old, was restored. Its story goes back to the seventh century, for legend has it that the Jampa Lhakhang of Bumthang and the Kyichu Lhakhang of Paro both belong to the twelve famous Buddhist temples erected at that time.

The Keys for the Future

Sindhu Râja, the story tells, was so very grateful for the help of Guru Rimpoché that he entrusted to him his most beautiful daughter, popularly called Princess Mön-mo. She was said to be an incarnation of a 'Cloud Fairy'. She was therefore in the position to be chosen as acolyte and

'Mystic Consort' of the Great Guru. The King turned to religious life and renounced all his earthly treasures, which Guru Rimpoché is said to have hidden for the future of the country. There are many tales of gold and jewels concealed behind rocks, in caves and in the depths of the lakes, but religious tradition stresses quite another kind of 'hidden treasure'. This is emphasised in the legend about the foundation of the 'Tiger-shaped Rock-Temple', situated by the river Tang Chu in the north of the Bumthang valley.

This small Rimocän Lhakhang stands at the foot and in the shadow of a haunted perpendicular rock-wall. High above it, in the rocks, bees have placed their honeycombs. The honey is collected, as depicted on stone-age drawings, by honey collectors sitting in baskets, which are let down on a rope from above. But on the rock-wall, just behind the temple, very small foot-prints are shown, which are said to have been those of a Tibetan princess, who, when only eight years old, accompanied Guru Rimpoché to Bumthang and died at this spot. Furthermore, it is related that the body of the princess was entombed in the rock together with scriptures containing precious advice, which could not be understood at that time. Thus scripts were immured in the rock, hidden for the benefit of the future, when the country might be in great danger again. So this rock-cave is reputed to contain the spiritual treasures called the 'Mystic Keys to the Future', but nothing other than the small footprints are to be seen on the gigantic rock-wall. This tiger-shaped rock, according to legend, was once a tiger demon who tried to attack Guru Rimpoché and was petrified by him. Pious pilgrims still see the tiger's shape in the rock.

Tales of Guru Rimpoché, the Lotus-born, dominate the holy places of Bumthang. His special memorial temple, the Kuje Lhakhang, as the name indicates, enshrines an impression of the person of the great converter. He had sat there in meditation in a rock-cave and the grotto later formed the altar niche of the temple which was built around it. A statue of Guru Rimpoché, larger than life, stands on the altar and behind, on the dark rock-wall, the impression is shown to the visitors. Below the temple is a small entrance to a natural rock-tunnel, connecting the Kuje Lhakhang with the monastery erected on the summit of the mountain. To prove the existence of this tunnel, the temple guardians put a cock into the entrance

28

on the hill, and afterwards a cat; it is said that both safely reached the lower outlet of the small tunnel. The big tree, in front of the Kuje Lhakhang, is reputed to have sprouted from a pilgrim's staff left behind by Guru Rimpoché.

The Festival in the Valley of the Swans

Guru Rimpoché, the saviour of Bumthang, is also connected with a cycle of legends woven around the Swan's Temple, Ngang Lhakhang, in the Valley of the Swans. It is situated on the upper course of the Camkhar Chu, north-west of Bumthang, at a spot once inhabited only by swans, hence its name. On his mission to the south, and after crossing many difficult passes, Guru Rimpoché arrived here and was immediately attacked by the demons of the woods. Desiring peace and quietness for his meditations, he started to kick stones at the trouble-makers; at first he pushed small stones, and later bigger ones, until the demons withdrew. So the village, which was later built on the spot, was called the 'Place of the Lotus-foot Impressions', because every stone touched by the Lotus-born miraculously showed the impression of his foot. The most beautiful of these stones is carefully kept as a precious relic in a dark shrine of a small temple.

Opposite that village, an hour's walk away, the Swan's Temple was erected in a later epoch. Every year, at the beginning of December, its foundation is celebrated with a religious festival and all the people from neighbouring regions come together to enjoy it. On the first day of the feast, at dawn, they arrive from every direction in single-file processions, traversing the narrow woodland paths, dressed as usual for such special occasions in new hand-woven clothes, happy to participate in rites that have been handed down from their golden age and fill them with rapturous delight.

Out of the crowd, now assembled behind the Temple of the Swan, the head lama emerges, seated on a white horse, led by monks. His dark red robe swings about his body; on his head is a shining tiara, and a small umbrella, of glittering yellow silk, mounted on a bamboo stick fifteen feet long, is always held high above his head. The formal march around the temple proceeds. The head lama, accompanied by his monks, is followed by the men of the villages, dressed in their long, dark blue knight's costumes, with colourful rings around their heads. All Bhutias, being free men and therefore bearing arms, thus maintain an old and precious tradition. The rest of the villagers, and the lay-dancers in normal costume, follow them closely. In front of the temple door the procession halts. Lamas and men disappear into the temple of the Protective Deities. There the lay-dancers, in a ritual ceremony, are provided with masks and costumes, and the knights receive their shields, helmets and swords. Thus adorned, they emerge again and proceed to the small temple court, where the head lama is seated under his yellow umbrella.

The first spectacle is the Sword Dance performed by the village headman, surrounded by the 'Hero Dancers' in their knightly armour. Every day this Sword Dance is the first and the last item in the performances which last three days. After the Sword Dance in the small court, the Hero Dancers—that is their name precisely—swarm out into the big court in front of the temple, opening the festival with round dances. Meanwhile, the villagers and their guests have settled partly around the stage-court and partly around the head lama, whose whereabouts are always marked by the yellow umbrella above his head. Giving blessings all around, he proceeds slowly to a special pavilion in the background of the court. From there he can watch the spectacle and, if he wants, can hide behind screens. The monks' orchestra is installed opposite the temple door, which is covered by two curtains. When the Hero Dancers have finished their round dances, the dancing-master takes over the court: swinging his staff, decorated with fluttering ribbons, he announces the beginning of the ritual dances.

Now, in the Himalayas at a height of over 12,000 feet, begins the very oldest display of folk-dancing. The first dancers, leaping through the curtains, introduce the spectacle. All the eight traditional mask-dances are performed. The four Cemetery Dancers, with skull masks, here as well as in Paro, warn everybody of the illusory nature of worldly pleasures. Eight masked dancers demonstrate with the Small Drums, and eight with the Big Drums drive away all evil. Eight unmasked dancers carry lances and wear helmets mounted with three-cornered flags. The famous Black Hat Dancers are not masked; they wear the enormous, broad-brimmed head-gear of the old shamanist magicians of Central Asia, which is topped   30 by a glittering ornament and peacock feathers. Swinging the ritual dagger, they perform a symbolic drama dance in which the effigy of the apostate king of the ninth century, Langdarma, who destroyed religion, is struck by an arrow, shot by a monk disguised as a 'black magician'. Clad in the long-sleeved costumes of the magicians, which reach down to the ground, the Black Hat Dancers whirl around so rapidly that their robes take on a cylindrical form, and the sand in the court rises in clouds. During the following Dance of the Great Assemblage, the dancers form a ring and, bowing their heads, receive bread and wine.

Most picturesque is the round-dance parade of the Cham-masks, the dancers wearing painted animal masks which enable them to see through the wide open mouths. They look, for instance, through the tusk-armed, open snout of a wild boar, or their eyes are to be seen peeping through the open jaws and nose of the antlered stag-masks, or the wide-open beaks of the bird-masks, reminding us of the guardian magicians, with feathered bird-shaped hats, described in the old annals as those who watched over the entrances to the tent-camps of the early Tibetan kings. The former heathen gods, now gloriously tamed and under oath to protect religion, wear skull-crowned masks, with a third eye in the forehead and a gaping mouth, ready to seize the enemies of religion. Therefore, no matter how wrathful they appear, they give the audience a thrilling and comforting exhibition.

The dancing-master is always in evidence: very alert, he helps to put a Black Hat in the right position, or he plucks a dancer by the sleeve, or he fixes a slipping mask. He directs the whole spectacle, swinging his staff and giving encouraging orders. Every evening the Hero Dancers perform their round-dances and the day's performance ends with the Sword Dance in the small temple court. Their voices ring out in song and their swords flash in the light of the fire which has been kindled for the night.

The Dance of Death

The ritual dances at the Swan's Temple are interesting not only for their primitiveness: they are old dance dramas, kept alive under the guidance of a wise head lama. On the third and last day of the festival there are five performances. As usual, the show begins in the early morning with the circumambulation of the temple, followed by the Hero Dances. The round-dances by the knights are followed by the 'Great Dance of the Lord of Death' surrounded by his Cemetery Guardians; it is a version of the *danse macabre,* allegorically demonstrating the universal fate of all living things. But in the Valley of the Swans this is only an introduction to the age-old Dance of Death, here performed in its most aboriginal way. The spectators sit watching breathlessly; the only sounds to be heard are those of the rolling drums, thundering trumpets and clashing cymbals. Then a single mask-dancer leaps out through the temple curtains, taking possession of the whole scene. He is clad only in a loin-cloth; skeleton-ribs are painted on his upper body, his face is covered by a death mask. He has to master the big stage-court alone, and he succeeds. As he performs his *danse macabre* the sand on the courtyard floor whirls up in clouds, and his shadow, in the sinking sun, follows him in fantastic display. He is an acrobat: he leaps high and he rolls in the dust; he stands on his hands, turns cart-wheels and throws hand-springs. Now he symbolically drums on a gazelle skin, gathers dust in it and, running around the whole place, throws the dust over the heads of the spectators, thus reminding them that all life is dust, doomed to decay and to vanish into nothingness. Then he returns to the centre of the scene, swinging a long bamboo pole; his shadow becomes longer. Suddenly, it seems from nowhere, the place is filled with a crowd of antlered Stag Dancers. They, too, are clad only in loin-cloths, but their heads are crowned by the gigantic, nodding antlers, adorned with flapping wings. They surround the skeleton-dancer in a menacing ring, but Death pursues them with his whip, while they try to pursue him, too. The antlered cannibal dancers again form a circle always attacked by Death, and are finally driven away. It is a confusing and ghostly show, which suddenly vanishes like a nightmare.

The Mask-play of the first Kings and Queens

This performance has, however, only cleared the scene for the next performance, a whole masked drama, known as 'The Mask-Dance of the First Fathers and Mothers', the *Phole Mole Cham*. It tells the story of the first two kings who, with their two queens, came from heaven to bring civilization to ignorant people. The actors fill the whole place. Male dancers play the rôles of the queens; they wear ancient wooden masks which cover their faces completely. Thus, not being able to look around through the small eye-holes, they have to be guided.

The first solemn act of this mask-play shows the royal marriage between the fully armed kings and the beautifully crowned queens, whose goggle-eyed, wooden faces are painted white, with rosy cheeks. This marriage ceremony is the great moment for the jesters to display their rustic humour; far from modest, and wildly acclaimed by the audience, they display their phallic symbols, emphasising their desire for fertility. The second act shows the difficulties of war in legendary times: the enemy is near, announced by messengers, and the kings must go away to fight for the country, and in a colourful ceremony the queens are invested with all the insignia of power to rule the country in the absence of the men. The Queen-Dancers, standing still, accept the gifts and honours that are showered upon them; they are weighed down by their masks and can hardly stir during the moving scenes enacted around them. In the next act, the kings having departed for the battlefield, barbarians charge in and carry off the queens on their shoulders; the abduction is accompanied by howls of protest from the crowd. It is a very ancient presentation of 'bridal robbery', the invaders eloping (this is the word used) with the beautiful queens in the absence of the warrior-kings. Act four is a sinister show: the victorious kings, returning home at last, find their country occupied by fiends and their queens abducted.

So the great battle begins. For this the whole stage is divided in half by a strong rope, held at each end by yelling jesters. The furious kings unsheath their long swords, and with resounding clashes cross them with enemy swords over the stretched rope. The spectators cheer or hiss the fighters, who form a mass of most picturesque masks as they thrust hither and thither, divided only by the swinging rope. The kings must be victorious, of course; nevertheless, the severity of the battle must be emphasised until at last the queens can be brought ceremonially back. But act five reveals a grand tribunal at which the queens are accused of having made things too easy for the fiends. Voices thunder and the accusers, accused, and all the witnesses do their best to dramatise the situation. The queens weep. The trial ends with a verdict of guilty, the queens are condemned to have the tips of their noses cut off, and with both actors and spectators yelling loudly, the sentence is carried out with a sweep of the longest sword. The scene has the full vividness worthy of an old drama: justice must take its course to clear the stage for the happy ending. Kings and queens, united again in peace, can proceed with their task of pacifying the country and leading it on its way to civilization.

This *Phole Mole Cham* ends in the twilight. It is followed by a final, charming mask-dance of the 'Cloud Fairies' who, walking in the air between heaven and earth, promise to guide human beings to a higher spiritual sphere. With the setting of the sun, the last mask disappears. The stage is cleared for the very last Hero Dances, which end the festival in the small court after nightfall, performed around a burning fire. The leader, a red pointed cap of goat's skin on his head, swings his shining sword for the last time to the rhythm of the songs that fill the night air.

The Story-telling Bard

Guru Rimpoché and the 'Hidden Treasures of Bumthang' were much commemorated at the beginning of the fifteenth century, during the life-time of Pämalingpa. He, the 'Son of the Lotus Grove', opened a new epoch, reviving the era of the 'Lotus-born'. He was venerated as the true incarnation of Guru Rimpoché, continuing his tradition 'with body, speech and mind'. It is quite an experience to see and to hear how the legends, woven around this most famous son of Bumthang, are still alive in Künzangda, the rock-monastery of the 'all-merciful Buddha'. It is built high into the rocks that rise above the birth-place of Pämalingpa, situated in the mountain chains to the north of Bumthang, one day's ride on horseback   34 from the Castle of the White Bird. We had to dismount before the steep rock and climb up slowly. On the balconies of the monastery, which over-hang the abyss, stood monks with their long trumpets: they blew the wel-come salute to the first women visitors from a foreign land. Their blasts lasted quite a while, because we took nearly an hour to reach them.

A cold wind blew around the rock-monastery, but the main altar-room radiated a strange warmth. Countless butter-lamps were burning in front of the altar, which was graced by a gigantic statue of Guru Rimpoché. Here he is depicted with his eyes looking musingly upwards, watching—so the legend says—his Mystic Consort flying through the air. She is one of the 'Cloud Fairies', or 'Sky Travellers', who show men the spiritual path to liberation from earthly suffering. In this altar-room, in the late evening, we all sat around the open fire-bowl with outstretched hands, warming them at the blaze. Hot butter-tea was served in small wooden bowls, just the right thing to create the necessary inner warmth. The glowing wood-fire and the flames of the butter-lamps spread a flickering light, in which the golden images glittered. In the Himalayas, too, evening is the time for story-telling and our bard had in fact followed us from the Castle of the White Bird. Here he sat and, looking very important, slowly took out of his breast-pocket a small print. His humorous eyes twinkled, because he already understood that these curious pilgrims from the western world always wanted everything written or printed on the original plant-fibre paper which in Bhutan is particularly fine. The print contained the beauti-ful life-story of Pämalingpa, who was one of the most famous 'treasure finders' of his time, an epoch which has vanished so completely that it sounds now like a fairy tale.

The legend of the foundation of Künzangda goes back to a 'pre-founda-tion', to the first blessing of the holy place by Guru Rimpoché's most popu-lar 'Mystic Consort', Yeshé Khado, the 'Fairy of Wisdom'. It is said that she came there with Guru Rimpoché on their mission to the Land of Mön. She was once a Tibetan village girl, who, on her own initiative, had studied the whole literature and history of Buddhism. She was therefore regarded as an incarnation of the 'Cloud Fairy of Wisdom'. The fame of her beauty and knowledge spread till it reached the ears of the great king who ruled in Lhasa and was so impressed by what he had heard that he wanted her to become his queen. But his messengers had no success at all: Yeshé Khado had no desire for a luxurious life and rejected the palace pleasures she was offered. Her mind was set upon religion, so she refused the king and ran away to hide in the mountain solitudes. Royal messengers were sent in search of her and after several months found her sitting in a cave, deeply absorbed in meditation. She was brought to Lhasa, but there she had the luck to meet Guru Rimpoché, who understood her serious intentions and saved her. He admitted her to the circle of his spiritual companions and took her with him on all his travels, including the journey to the Land of Mön.

Three famous monasteries in Bhutan claim the honour that their holy places were blessed by Yeshé Khado, not only Künzangda in Bumthang, but also the temple of Sengge Dzong in Kurtö, and Taktshang, the Tiger's Den monastery near Paro, which originally was founded as a convent. All these legendary foundations were like Kuje Lhakhang in that they were originally just the holy places or grottos where the saintly personages meditated, worked miracles, cured the sick and spread the first Buddhist blessings. The temples and monastery buildings were added later and were restored and enlarged periodically in order to do honour to the holy places.

The Dream Vision of Pämalingpa

The birth-place of Pämalingpa is situated below the rocks of Künzangda. His life-story still has the magic charm of the vanished shamanistic world from which he emerged to become the native Buddhist Guru of Bumthang. Pämalingpa is reputed to have had a dwarf-like figure; originally he was a blacksmith, a craft in which the Bhutanese were famous throughout Central Asia. Bhutanese swords and coats of mail were highly prized, and the matchless Bhutanese bell-founding was praised everywhere.

On the day Pämalingpa, the dwarf-like smith, reached the age of twenty-seven, he went into the forest to look for mushrooms, but found none. On his way back he met a hermit with a long white beard and spoke to him full of respect, sadly mentioning that he could not offer him a meal because he had not found a single mushroom. The hermit smiled, bowed

36

and with his hands pushed aside the twigs that were lying on the ground, revealing a whole bed of wonderful mushrooms. Pämalingpa collected them and invited the old man to the meal. When they arrived at the hut, Pämalingpa cooked the mushrooms with five kinds of fragrant herbs and, when they were ready, called for the hermit. But the hermit was no longer there; he seemed to have disappeared. Pämalingpa called him again and searched everywhere in vain. Finally, and sadly, he ate the delicious mushrooms alone. Afterwards he climbed to the roof of his hut, lay down and musingly watched the clouds sweeping over the sky. Then he remembered that the hermit had given him a small paper-roll, which he took from his pocket and studied ponderingly. He had not learned to read, but intuitively he grasped the deeper meaning of the written message—or had it been whispered into his ear? 'Go to the Burning Lake! There you will find a hidden treasure!' For the message was written in the so-called 'fairy script', derived from the Devanagari script of the Gods, which only a few scholars from the Old Sect, the Nyingmapa, were able to read. Pämalingpa understood more with his heart than with his mind, and it began to dawn on him that the hermit might have been a manifestation of Guru Rimpoché, who showed himself in this form in order to receive Pämalingpa as his own true incarnation. Thus, according to the legend, Pämalingpa realized that he was in fact the embodiment of the Lotus-born Precious Guru.

The Legend of the Burning Lake

On the first night of the full moon, following this event, Pämalingpa, the tiny man of the Lotus Grove, accompanied by his relatives, proceeded to the Burning Lake. This lake, still known today, is hidden in the densest part of the highland forest to the east of Künzangda. In Pämalingpa's day many people reported having seen flickering lights on the surface, and the name derived from this report; all superstitious people avoided approaching the place. But the fearless Pämalingpa, having arrived at the lake with his relatives, leaped upon a rock on the shore and stared at the dark and quiet surface of the water on which the full moon was mirrored.

He had no idea how to fulfil his task or how to reach the bottom of the lake.

Suddenly, he heard a whistling wind and felt as if he were pulled downwards in an 'air-bell' till he stood before a temple with many doors, only one of which was open. Before this door was an old and ugly woman with a wrathful face, with only one eye and one long protruding tooth, who told him that Guru Rimpoché had left for him a small casket. Pämalingpa was filled with fear because he had no idea how to get back to the surface of the lake; but again he heard the whistling sound and felt himself carried upwards and out of the lake. At last he stood again on the rock at the lake shore, holding the casket in his hands. Without uttering a word, Pämalingpa and his relatives returned home. On the way they passed a small temple. Pämalingpa slipped in and stayed there, and from that night he has been known everywhere as 'Pämalingpa, the Treasure Finder', and people began to recall that, even as a small boy, Pämalingpa had behaved strangely and spoken of himself as an incarnation of Guru Rimpoché.

The Heavenly Flowers

Pämalingpa's uncle knew that his nephew had found a spiritual treasure in the Burning Lake and that he must be the true incarnation of the Lotusborn, and so he wished to celebrate the great event with the whole family and with the people of the village. But Pämalingpa still stayed away, hiding himself in the small temple, because he did not know how to preach religion, having learnt nothing and never having had a teacher. One night he sat in the altar room praying and invoking the power of his spiritual father, when suddenly he fell asleep and in a vision saw the heavenly 'Cloud Fairies' before him, teaching him the fundamental principles of all the religions of the world. Thus, sleeping in the temple with the casket in his arms, the Buddhist teachings became manifest to him. The casket itself was filled with small script-rolls, on which, in 'fairy script', the words of the Buddha were recorded.

It was in his dream vision that Pämalingpa was initiated into his future task and was given the power to find the right word at the right moment for the right purpose. He began to preach the very next morning. The villagers gathered around him in wonderment and listened to his words, and while he spoke beautiful flowers, in all the colours of the rainbow, fell from the sky. But nobody could catch them, for they vanished like rays of light into nothingness.

This is 'The Story of the Heavenly Flowers' and of the first preaching of the treasure-finder Pämalingpa, kept alive today in the oral tradition. At the beginning of his religious life Pämalingpa, who had been a smith, took an oath that he would never again enter a forge, and he sealed his anvil with the imprint of his small foot. This anvil is the most precious relic of Künzangda and is shown to all pilgrims in the shrine above the main temple.

The Tears of a Disciple

At the time of Pämalingpa an evil chieftain ruled over the district to the east of the Burning Lake, and was so powerful that his influence began to reach Bumthang. When we heard about the treasure-finder he was consumed with a raging desire to possess the treasure which, like many people, he understood only in the material sense of the word, as a question of gold and jewels. He ordered Pämalingpa to bring him the treasures from the Burning Lake, and the pious man raised his warning voice in vain, trying to explain that the right moment to draw up the hidden treasures of that special kind had not yet come. The chieftain only became more angry and eventually forced Pämalingpa to accompany him to the lake.

It was a strange procession trough the dense woods: the evil chieftain with his retinue of wild warriors, and Pämalingpa, the saintly man, followed by his disciples. The moment they reached the shores of the Burning Lake, Pämalingpa, without fear, stepped onto the surface of the water. The waves embraced him, but this time there was no whistling wind to be heard, but a raging storm that sucked Pämalingpa down. The disciples, seeing how their Guru had disappeared into the lake, began to pray fervently. Only the very youngest among them could not endure it and out of fear for his admired Guru began to cry. At last the waters opened again and

Pämalingpa stepped upon the shore untouched by them. The chieftain's followers searched him all over, but his robes were dry, with the exception of one small lappet which had been wet by the tears of the youngest disciple. Pämalingpa remained silent as he held a sealed box in his hands. In a voice of thunder the chieftain ordered him to open it. Now Pämalingpa spoke, explaining that the time to unveil the hidden treasures, still completely misunderstood, had not yet come. Instead of an answer, the mighty chieftain, in a fury, flourished his sword and with one stroke cut the box in half. But only a cloud of smoke escaped from it and a husky voice was heard, predicting that Pämalingpa would soon die and that the chieftain with all his family, his retinue and his treasures would become extinct. And indeed, shortly afterwards, the avaricious man was conquered by the Hero of Ura and all his accumulated worldly treasures were destroyed.

This Hero of Ura was called 'Black Devil' and he is said to have built the highland road of rocks and stones which leads from eastern Bumthang over Ura and three difficult passes to the old Dzong of Zhonggar. We rode along this narrow road, which must once have been a masterpiece of medieval road building; the stone-slabs are still in their places, but the old Castle of Zhonggar, to-day hidden behind jungles, is a complete ruin.

White Stupas of the East

The actual district centre east of Bumthang is Mongar Dzong. To reach it along the old road, several high passes have to be crossed. First of all it traverses the rock-road built by the Hero of Ura. The traffic of past ages must have been quite developed, because stone-roads of this kind spread far to the east and north-east beyond the present boundaries of Bhutan. Both men and horses must climb over the passes, the first of which is the Rodung La. Then the road descends to the foot of the Wangthang La. The top of this pass is reached over ice-covered rivulets, with a view which is even more beautiful than that from the Dochu La in Western Bhutan: a complete view of the imposing ice-covered frontier of Bhutan, stretching like a diamond necklace along the northern horizon. Down again, and up again over the

Thumseng La, to find a resting-place at Senggor Lhakhang. Up again before dawn, and over the Datong La to reach the central farm of Lingmething, rich in maize-fields. Behind them, in the densest mountain jungle, the ruins of Zhonggar Dzong are hidden.

We now arrived at the river Kuru Chu, thundering down from north to south. Already between the Säling Chu, and before reaching the Kuru Chu, we had seen small reliquaries built in the style of the Indian stupas of the Emperor Ashoka, also to be seen in Nepal. The first of them stands in the dense woods beyond Cändänbi, on the way to Tongsa Dzong, but here, in the region of the Kuru Chu, the path is flanked by them in every size. Above the four square bases, one above the other, facing the four cardinal points, curves the big cupola, and above this cupola the eyes of the Mystic Buddha watch on all four sides. The cupola culminates in the 'Steps of Enlightenment', which narrow to a point and once ended in a double emblem of sun and moon together—the eternal symbol of the 'Twin-unity of Contrasts'. But there are also smaller stupa-like chörtens without the watching eyes of the Buddha and without the topmost symbols. There are different Bhutanese stupas, some of them almost in ruins, others freshly white-washed, with engraved images painted over in colour. The biggest and most beautiful of these reliquaries, also called 'eye chörtens', with the all-seeing eyes of the Mystic Buddha darkly painted, was erected in far eastern Bhutan, to the north of Tashiyangtse. Another of these stupas, so unexpected in these eastern Himalayan regions, towers above the banks of the Kuru Chu, below Mongar Dzong. These stupas, still enshrining the secrets of their foundations, are the religious and architectural symbols of East Bhutan. According to the oral tradition, Guru Rimpoché introduced this special kind of stupa into Bhutan. Guru Rimpoché, according to legend, in one of his former lives, was one of the builders of the Great Stupa at Bodhnath, near Kathmandu in Nepal.

Eros and Psyche in the Bhutanese Himalayas

Mongar Dzong, the new district centre, is still immersed in the sagas and legends of the old Zhongar Dzong, by which it is connected to the monasteries of Pämalingpa. We hardly dared trust our ears when we heard here a Himalayan version of one of the most well-known fairy-tale motifs of antiquity. For here we met the Psyche of Zhongar and Eros. In the temple of the protective Deities of Mongar Dzong, to the left and to the right of the altar, two life-size guardians stand rigid, with mask-like faces painted in the manner of old wooden full-masks and with protruding eyes. The gorgeously dressed statues represent the aboriginal local guardian deities of the place: a gigantic warrior, fully armed, and a lovely maiden, clad in the old national costume and wearing a golden crown. They are the hero and heroine of local legend. He is the mountain god Daktsän, one of the pre-Buddhist Tsän-gods, said to live in the spere between earth and sky. Long ago this mountain god fell in love with the fairest girl of the village and every night he visited her in the shape of a young man, but before dawn he always hurried away. The girl, Pänchen Zangmo, could not imagine how her lover would look in daylight, and when she could no longer bear this uncertainty she laid her plans. The next night she put a big ball of thread beside her bed and before her lover left her she managed to fasten one end of the thread to his foot. Then she simulated sleep. But the moment he slipped away, she jumped out of her bed and followed him at a distance, always holding the ball of thread in her hand. In the dark he crossed the village and took to the hill-side; it was a long way, but at last he reached a big cave which the villagers knew to be haunted. The girl, carefully winding up the thread, anxiously peeped into the cave, which was now somewhat lightened by the coming dawn, but all she could see was a gigantic dragon-snake, a horrible demon, to whose left hind-foot her thread was still attached. The poor girl was so terrified that she fainted away and died. The demon god, in utter desperation, guarded the dead body of the girl. Breathing fire, he would not allow anyone to come near, and the villagers did not know what to do. Finally they remembered the famous lamas of the monasteries of Pämalingpa in Bumthang. They sent a messenger over the three difficult passes begging for help. A lama arrived and fearlessly went to the cave, sat down and stayed in deep meditation at the feet of the dragon-demon, who still watched the body of his bride. But the lama patiently used his religious power, dedicated to the benefit of all beings, and at last the demon was pacified and took an oath that henceforward he would fight only for religion. The lama blessed both him and Pänchen Zangmo and transformed them into guardian deities who, together again, had to stand guard before the veiled altar of the Protective Deities of Mongar Dzong.

This story, transferred from the old Zhongar Dzong to Mongar and with even older roots, is typical of the popular conversion legends in which the former heathen deities were symbolically conquered, so that, with the direction of their activities changed, they were newly installed as 'oath-bound fighters' for the Buddhist faith. Bloody struggles were transformed into peaceful conversions, and blood sacrifices (formerly usual) became symbolic offerings. In this way the population did not lose their old gods who, on the contrary, acquired new importance through their help in driving away every hindrance to the path of religion.

The Frescoes of Bumthang

Pätshälling Gömpa, the 'Lotus-grove Monastery', lies in a sunny hollow in the mountains north of the ruins of the Iron Castle in Bumthang. Its site was ideally chosen. On the north it is protected by rising mountain walls and to the south it is open to the sun. There, up in the hills, it is warm even if down in the valley an icy wind assaults the walls of the Castle of the White Bird. Pätshälling Gömpa is surrounded by cyprus and sandalwood trees. Between them grow rhododendrons and juniper-bushes. Today it is only a place of pilgrimage, guarded by a caretaker. The walls of the temple of the Protective Deities are decorated with most beautiful old weapons and buckler-shields covered by rhino skin. The altar niche is a big, completely veiled, phurbu-shrine, the centre of which consists of 108 phurbus forming a mandala pattern.

The phurbus, usually described as ritual daggers, are really nails, ritual nails of an archaic shape, ending in an ornamented, blunt, triangular point, and crowned by the four heads of a protective deity. With these dagger-nails the old heathen gods were banished and symbolically nailed to the ground. Phurbus were the 'twelve nails' by which, according to tradition, the gigantic heathen demoness was nailed down at all the main points of Central Asia and the Himalayas. These phurbus marked the sites of the first twelve Buddhist shrines already referred to, which were erected early in the seventh century, two of these holy places being claimed by Bhutanese tradition. Made of bronze or of wood, the dagger-nails are also swung during the ritual dances to announce symbolically that malevolent demons have been nailed down.

One of the most important of Pämalingpa's foundations is the 'Temple of the Merry Message', the Tamshing Lhakhang. At present the young incarnation of Pämalingpa resides there, educated and lovingly cared for by monks from Lhalung. In the hall of the main temple, a precious relic of Pämalingpa is shown: a heavy coat of mail once forged by the saint himself before he was initiated. In his religious life, during meditation, he had to cover himself with this heavy piece of armour 'to avoid being lifted into the air'. The whole temple is built strictly proportionate to the stature of this saint of dwarf-like shape. The doorways are so low that visitors often butt their foreheads against the upper frame, but they are warned against this special feature of the architecture displayed in honour of the founder.

Tamshing has three temple halls. The first is dedicated to Guru Rimpoché, the second to the Buddha of Eternal Light, and the third is the secret temple of the Protective Deities. Here the frescoes are painted upon a shining black background. They look like a fierce procession of wrathful deities covered with a thousand eyes, riding surrounded by flames, many-headed, the lower parts of their bodies being the coiled tails of snakes. These wrathful gods, depicted in their tantric aspects, belong to the planetarian circle, watching all points of the universe; however terrifying their appearance pious people are not afraid because all these frightening aspects are directed against the enemies of religion only. Paradise, the frescoes show, is guarded by a bizarre couple of Skeleton Dancers, reminding us of the fact that even the gods and paradise are only a transient conception, and that the spiritual realm of final liberation is to be found on another level, in the formless sphere that lies beyond all earthly imagination.

44

Pätshälling abounds in beautiful frescoes. The paintings on the walls be-hind the big temple hall belong to a heavenly sphere. They have a universal appeal. The background is red-brown and the Buddhas, Bodhisattvas and saints are painted finely and lightly, seeming to float on their lotus thrones, surrounded by double haloes. Their smiling faces transmit a strange kind of quiescence. The temple frescoes of Bhutan, from the cosmic mandalas of Paro Dzong to the precious frescoes in the eastern part of the country, are among the greatest treasures of Buddhist art, but they are also very delicate and are endangered by the severe climate of the country. The winter's cold and the summer fogs have had serious effects upon these treasures, and also upon the wooden framework of the buildings. Enormous trouble is taken to repair, to preserve and to enlarge the buildings, but the paintings are sometimes simply over-painted with new motifs. But this itself is part of a religious ritual to bring them alive again. It is also usual every year to whitewash the chörtens and to repaint the semi-reliefs on the slate plates, all of which work is done primarily to emphasise the vitality of the images; for it must be remembered that for all those—and this means the majority of people—who need pictures, like steps of a ladder, to help them climb from the earthly sphere of suffering to the spiritual realms beyond, pictures are no more than 'thinking-tools', instruments necessary to stir the divine power in human beings and enable them eventually to reach a sphere where pictures will no longer be necessary. This all-embracing concept is the greatest mystery, but it is inherent, though mostly unconsciously so, in the heart of the most simple-minded of these people, who feel spontaneously the Buddhist message that the 'potential Nirvana', or divine spark, is inborn in every living being.

The Temple of the Broken Bell

The legends woven around the holy places of Bumthang have always a historic kernel. There is a temple, the Konchogsum Lhakhang, which is said to have been founded in the time of Guru Rimpoché. It is popularly called 'Temple of the Broken Bell'. Bell-founding has already been mentioned as the pride and the secret of the Bhutanese bronze-workers. One of their prototype bells is a masterpiece now preserved in the Konchogsum Lhak-hang. It sounded so beautiful, so legend has it, that it could not have been cast by men. It was a gift from a Nâga princess, one of the water-spirits, the lower parts of whose bodies have the form of a snake, and who are said to be the guardians of the Books of Wisdom. This famous bell rang so clearly and so loudly that it even could be heard in Lhasa on the Roof of the World. Thisongdetsän, the great king who then reigned, at the end of the eighth century, became envious. He, too, wanted to have such a wonderful bell. So he sent mounted troops to the south-eastern Himalayas, with the order to bring that bell back with them. But the bell was so heavy that even the strongest among the Tibetan soldiers were not able to lift it even an inch. Therefore, with all their strength they tried to break it into pieces, so that its sound could no more 'offend' the ears of the King.

This is the story of the precious relic of 'The Temple with the Broken Bell', which is supplemented by other traditions. From the highest temple tower of the Castle of the White Bird a battlefield is shown where, it is said, some Tibetan warriors marched in. The lamas, in great haste, assembled in the temple of the Protective Deities, where they prayed so fervently, invoking the help of divine power, that all the weapons, including a huge medieval cannon, went off by themselves and chased the unwanted visitors away. Similar legends are told everywhere in these regions.

Fifteen Districts and Fifteen Languages

In the oldest written records the whole terrain of present-day Bhutan was called 'The Four Districts of Southern Mön'. It was then the retreat of the Mönpas, who once were spread all over the Himalayan regions and whose language is still alive today in the south-eastern districts of Bhutan. Along the old caravan roads through Paro in the west and Tashigang in the east, trade and traffic has gone on since time immemorial and the produce of the north—salt, musk, wool and textiles—was bartered in the bazaars to the south, at the foot of the Himalayas. The route from Paro led to Pasamkha, which is marked as 'Buxa' on our maps, a name which has an amusing history, for it derives from the British transcription of the word *baksheesh,* used by Moslem traders and meaning 'tip'. The British of those days were fanatical horse lovers and were deeply offended by the Bhutanese habit of cutting the long bushy tails of their mountain horses as soon as they arrived at Pasamkha, because in the damp hot climate of the Terrai the horses, accustomed to mountain air, sweated profusely. The British offered large tips, *baksheesh,* to save the horses from what they regarded as degradation. So it became usual for the Bhutanese to expect this tip as a kind of right, and in the many dialects spoken at this trading centre, 'Buxa' finally became its internationally accepted name.

For travellers from the north Bhutan was the 'Paradise of the South'. In old texts it is even called the 'Lotus-grove of the Gods, rich in forests of sandalwood and fragrant medicinal herbs'. Bhutanese herbs, indeed, were always in great demand, and Himalayan herbs were already included in the prescriptions of the physicians of ancient India.

To Indians this country was simply known as 'The Land of the Bhutias', out of which the name Bhutan eventually developed. Some of the Bhutias, a name used in north-eastern India for all people of Tibetan descent, had already begun to settle within Bhutan's present boundaries in the seventh century, of which the four southernmost districts of Mön were well known. To the north, it was said, lay Punakha, 'The Blooming Vale of the Luxuriant Fruits of the South', the region where mandarins, bananas and big citrus-fruits grow, together with sugar cane and bamboo, surrounded by dense forests of fir, with orchids clinging to the branches of the trees. To the south lay Pasamkha, already mentioned, 'The Goal of all Desires' for traders and travellers. To the west lay Dalikha, 'The Region of Walnut Trees', known today as Kalimpong, which once belonged to Western Bhutan. To the east lay Dungsamkha, 'The Land of Longing and of the Silver Pines': now a bazaar at the end of the south-eastern highway.

Bhutan is divided into fifteen districts, which grew harmoniously out of history and tradition and were sheltered by the mountain ranges. This geographic pattern of fertile valleys surrounded by mountains gives the background to the whole administrative and political concept of the country. The mountain passes are the links between the inhabited valleys, which in the northernmost parts of the country, like Lunana, are cut off by snow and practically inaccessible during the winter.

When a traveller crosses a pass, comes to the first hamlet of the new district and speaks to the first inhabitant he meets, he is immediately aware that he is faced with a new dialect which has been kept alive through the ages in the seclusion of village life. Only two districts of Bhutan form part of the Terrai, the jungle region at the foot of the Himalayas, bordering the Indian plain, from which the mountains rise abruptly. It is here, in the south, that the jungle territories of the Manas River lie. The Manas is a mighty stream, rising in the northern mountains and carrying its torrents to the Indian south—the retreat of tigers and elephants and, farther east, of rhinos. Once a year, in winter, a royal safari is held at Manas, though otherwise hunting is not the custom of the country. The object of this single hunt is the tiger, regarded as a deadly threat to all other animals. This secluded part of the Bhutanese southern jungle then becomes alive: bamboo huts are quickly put up to give shelter to the hunting party, the tiger is traced, and finally, before dawn, shot from a 'hunting nest', a screened shooting platform built in a tree. The hunters and their retinue, sometimes six of them, form quite a picture as they sit on the back of an elephant, who proves his ability to stalk on every type of terrain. The hunting elephants can cross rivers, and they trample down the jungle growth in their path, thus demonstrating that they must have been the 'tanks' of past ages. Sometimes they stop suddenly as if hypnotised, lifting their trunks and trumpeting: only a python can frighten them in this way, a snake which is difficult to see when lying along a small brook and not easy to observe, anyway, by reason of its camouflage.

The other thirteen districts of Bhutan comprise the mountain regions from west to east, now being connected by new mountain roads. With their characteristic centres—the Bhutanese fortresses called dzongs—they represent the secular power as well as the religious tradition of the country. These old fortified castles, big enough to shelter hundreds, sometimes thousands, of people, survive into our times from the Middle Ages. Once they were important, providing the inner and outer security of Bhutan; they are still the residences of the district governors and the seats of the law courts. The National Assembly once met in the big 'Hall of the Thousand Buddhas' in Paro Dzong, its walls painted with a thousand Buddha images; but now that the new buildings of Thimphu Dzong are finished, the National Assembly has its home in the capital. The fortresses are all built according to a 48 general pattern, handed down since time immemorial. But this architecture is adapted to the natural surroundings. The dzongs are square buildings with tapering walls; they were erected at strategical points, either as mountain fortresses, seeming to have grown out of the spur of the mountain and dominating the whole valley, or they were built at the confluences of rivers. The variety of their architecture comes from the fact that the ground-plan was always adapted to the natural environment; thus they look as if grown out of earth and rock, becoming a harmonious part of the landscape. The Bhutanese, indeed, are the worthy heirs of the oldest Central Asian fortress builders.

Zhabdung, the Great Dukpa Founder

The most ancient fortress of Bhutan is Simthoka Dzong, situated in the south of the Thimphu Valley. It was erected in 1619 by the founder of Bhutan, Zhabdung I. It became a model for all other fortifications, and was the first monument to the sovereign rule of the religious Dharma Rajas and the secular Deb Rajas, a 'twin government' symbolic of theocratic rule. Zhabdung I, the first Dharma Raja, who symbolized the twin government in personal union, was not only the founder of Bhutan: he also impressed his religious zeal upon the country. A monk of the Dukpa sect, he represented for his followers the highest incarnation of the Dukpa line of the Bhutanese south-east. They were called 'Dukpa', 'Thunderers' or 'People of the Thunder-Dragon' because legend has it that during the erection of their earliest monastery, Duk Ralung in southern Tibet, a thunderstorm arose which threatened its walls. Bhutan participates in this founder-legend, because it is said that the big marble pillars for the temple were 'flown in' from the south-east, an expression which is by no means extravagant for a founder legend dating from the twelve century; for at that time saints and miracle workers, known to be able to overcome natural physical laws by their psychic strength, were greatly in vogue. The native name of the country, Dukyü, Land of the Thunderbolt-Dragon or Land of the Thunderers, can be explained by another version of the legend. Both names are correct. The Great Seal of Bhutan depicts two thunder-dragons encircling two crossed thunderbolts. This 'thunderbolt-cross' is a symbol of diamond-clear wisdom. On the popular level the thunder-dragon represents thunder and lightning associated with fertility-bringing rain; on the philosophical level, the dragon is the promulgator of absolute truth, which he proclaims in a thunderous voice.

But from the seventh century onwards followers of the Old Sect, the Nyingmapa, venerating Guru Rimpoché as their Mahaguru, came to Bhutan, followed by adherents of the Sakyapa. Not to be forgotten are the followers to the Kagyüpa Sect, the mother-school of the Dukpa, who also began to settle in western parts of Bhutan, into which Zhabdung I, the Great Dukpa, entered eventually over the Lingzhi Pass and impressed the religious tradition of his Dukpa chool.

Stepping into a New Epoch

During the many centuries of the theocratic rule of the Zhabdung Dynasty, which proceeded in a series of incarnations, the two 'penlops', the governors of Paro and Tongsa, became the mightiest men in the country. Around 1900 the Zhabdung incarnations came to an end and the more powerful penlop took the initiative. He was the Lord of Tongsa, Urgyän Wangchuck, who in 1907 was unanimously elected hereditary king. A new epoch opened for Bhutan under a wise king, who was a born diplomat and very able to protect his country, a small land sandwiched between two colossi, Tibet in the north and India in the south. Not only was he fully recognised by the British, then in power still in India, but he was granted a British title. Sir Urgyän, the crowned King of Bhutan, managed not only to stay on friendly terms with his southern neighbours, but he also handled all the very complicated frontier disputes concerning the southern Terrai districts; he secured the independence of his country and kept all foreign influence at a distance. There was not even a permanent British Resident in Bhutan and diplomatic contacts had to be dealt with by the British representative in Sikkim. This situation was rather unique, but obviously satisfactory to both sides. But in the Indo-Bhutanese Treaty there is a paragraph concerning international law which ensured mutual understanding in matter of foreign

50

policy. This paragraph was important for Bhutanese sovereignty, because Chinese troops—imperial troops at that time—threatened Lhasa and seemed intent on violating Bhutan's northern frontier.

Sir Claude White, the British diplomat and enthusiastic friend of the Bhutanese, was invited to Urgyän Wangchuck's coronation, which was celebrated with great pomp in the royal winter residence at Punakha. For this reason it was on some maps indicated as the Bhutanese capital, but the first diplomatic travellers, like G. Brogle and S. Turner, always referred to Thimphu, with the Tashichö Dzong, as the capital. The practice of having a 'winter residence' is still usual among the Bhutias, for in the coldest months—December and January, now the season of the long school holidays—many people, whole families, complete with servants and their entire possessions, proceed by horse caravan to southerly places. From the northernmost regions the herdsmen, too, and their yaks move south; and the people of northern Tang migrate to Bjakar Dzong, which, relative to their own mountain abodes, has a quite mild climate. People from Bumthang also go south.

Be that as it may, Punakha became known as the royal winter residence, and with the beginning of the reign of King Urgyän Wangchuck, nearly seventy years ago, the first seeds were sown of a new era in Bhutan. All the treaties concluded at that time were taken over by India and enlarged to include development aid. In 1958 Jawaharlal Nehru, then President of India, required nine whole days to cover the seventy miles to Western Bhutan by horse caravan, but in 1970 the Indian President, V. V. Giri, and his wife flew to Thimphu for a great state visit, arriving by helicopter at the Thimphu helipad and returning by car to Puntsholling, at the end of the south-western Bhutanese highway, which they reached in one day. This important state visit took place at an important moment, for India was sponsoring the motion to make Bhutan a member of the United Nations.

A Sealed Country opens its Doors

Bhutan has remained a 'sealed' country since its foundation. It was almost inaccessible to explorers, not to speak of tourists. During 300 years, from 1626 to 1921, only thirteen European expeditions reached Bhutan, and all but one were British. The other was accomplished by two Portuguese Fathers, St Cacella and J. Cabral, who in 1626 were the first Europeans to cross Western Bhutan. They stayed in Paro and Thimphu, cordially welcomed as 'Pandits from the far western world', but their fascinating report on the peaceful reign of Zhabdung I was never published. They experienced an astonishing degree of Buddhist tolerance, with no prejudice of any kind, but with respect for all other religions. The Bhutanese recognised their foreign religion as another path to liberation, adapted to the conditions of another land and another society, an attitude which was then and still is something new. Nothing was expected in return but equal tolerance and respect. For Europeans at that time, quite unaware of the fundamental principles of Buddhism, this was all quite puzzling.

George Brogle was the first British diplomat to reach Thimphu. He arrived there in 1774 to discuss the basic conditions for a treaty on Indo-Bhutanese trade and commerce. Carefully studying land and people, he became an ardent friend of the Bhutanese. The words he found to describe the Bhutanese are still most applicable today. As George Brogle put it, among a population that knows nothing of privileges of birth or the distinctions of clothing, since all of them, from the King to the farmer and servant, dressed the same, there could be no hauteur. The more George Brogle saw of the Bhutanese the more he liked them. He described the people as openhearted, good-humoured and trustworthy, but he realised that Bhutanese politicians knew very well the arts of diplomacy. He furthermore called the Bhutanese the best-looking people among the Himalayan mountaineers. He wrote in conclusion a beautiful farewell message to these honest and simple people, to whom he wished the long-lasting happiness that was already denied to the peoples of the technically developed nations which were blinded—so he said—by the restless pursuit of material gain. Thanks to Brogle's report, and its confirmation by those who followed him, Bhutan was protected from foreign influence and could strengthen its inner forces.

Three British missions between 1905 and 1907 were led by Sir Claude White, to the great satisfaction of both parties. Only since 1952 have the closed doors of that 'paradise of the south-eastern Himalayas' begun to open. At first, friends of the royal family had the opportunity to visit the country, and during the past few years small expeditions were allowed to enter. Swiss geologists, Japanese botanists and English biologists have studied the country and enriched their own field of knowledge, offering the product of their research to Bhutan. For a Tibetologist the crossing of this country has special attractions: everywhere, and especially in the unexplored far eastern districts, one finds places previously known only by names in old prints. Till now they have been legendary places, not to be localised, such as the Burning Lake, which is surrounded by a still living tradition. The story of the Iron Castle of Bumthang, with its historic background, sheds a new light on the accomplishments of the old Buddhist missionaries and their untiring travels up and down the difficult mountain passes. In this way we discovered Bhutan as a 'land of hidden treasures', its full spiritual value still to be uncovered and its abundant wealth in folklore still to be studied. Unfortunately, most of the Bhutanese printing blocks have been destroyed by fire, but there must be masses of prints still undiscovered in private libraries and in the store-rooms of the monasteries; they will help to fill the gaps in the early history of these people who, since the seventh century, have been busy recording events in manuscript, and who shortly afterwards began to print with engraved wooden blocks. The principal Bhutanese printing places, like Punakha and Simthoka, had been well known among those who read the classical Tibetan characters; they cherished books like holy images, wrapping them in silk and depositing them in altar niches. In this connection the wildly rumoured 'analphabetism' must be explained more carefully. In former times, and till very recently, it was usual that young boys and men spent several years in a monastery, in those days the only existing centres of education, to assist and to learn the fundamentals of their Buddhist culture. So one can find many old people, by no means scribes, who nevertheless can read the printed script. To-day all schools are free to all children, and school materials, such as pencils, paper and books, are free too. The pupils learn three languages from Bhutanese and Indian teachers, English being the third of them, and the Himalayan youngsters seem to be able to do this. They are most alert and have all the tradition of tolerance already referred to, which seems almost inborn in all Bhutias. It is a fact difficult to explain, but it clearly makes possible the acquisition of new techniques and ways of living without discarding the traditional background.

To-day new buildings, schools and hospitals are springing up in the Land of the Thunder-Dragon. Since 1961 they have been financed by Indian aid and they were built simultaneously with the new mountain roads. In 1962 Bhutan became a member of the Colombo Plan for Cooperative Economic Development in South and South-east Asia, and in 1968 Bhutan sent her first diplomatic observers to the United Nations; thus India's motion to make her a member of the United Nations acquired greater actuality. To-day, Bhutan has 800,000 inhabitants, living on 47,000 square kilometres; they speak fifteen dialects, with Dzongkha, the 'Dzong language', taught in all schools, as the common speech. Among a population scattered over great distances in the small valleys, the road to school might mean a march of many hours, so some of the schools have living accommodation for pupils during the week, the week-ends being spent at home. Because of the severe climate the long vacation has to be fixed during the coldest months. Although we travelled in winter, we were able to see some of the last days of school before the vacation at Cändänbi, a small village west of Tongsa. Punctually at seven in the morning the class-room was filled with pupils, beginning to recite Bhutanese texts.

The Sword-Dance

We arrived at Cänbänbi in the evening, unannounced, and found the lower part of the village deserted. Checking at the schoolhouse, where we were supposed to take up our quarters in one of the unoccupied school-rooms, we heard nothing and nobody was to be seen. Soon we learned that a great ceremony was about to take place on the hill in the upper village. All the inhabitants had assembled there on the village green. Night was falling, so we hurried there and arrived just in time to enjoy a unique spectacle of traditional country life. On one side of the village green a half-opened

54

tent had been put up in which, on a high cushion, the village lama was enthroned. Dignitaries crowded round him. Flanking the open place, in the first row, the schoolchildren sat cross-legged, clad in their dark blue Bhutanese school-dress, which is cut like the Bhutanese national male dress; with shining eyes they awaited the great performance. Behind them the villagers, obviously with guests from neighbouring hamlets, were crowded together. Meanwhile, many men had accumulated in the tent, or were rushing in and out, preparing a big fire in the middle of the square.

Suddenly, a man of imposing stature emerged from the tent and in a very dignified fashion proceeded towards the middle of the square. This was the village chieftain, clad in the ancient dress of a Sword Dancer. He looked around proudly, ready to perform one of the oldest forms of the warrior dance. Standing there solemnly, a figure unchanged through the ages, unrefined and aboriginal, he dominated the scene. He was the only actor. He wore the dark blue robe of the old warriors, long, wide and swinging, encircled by a heavy sword-belt. On his head he wore a pointed cap, four feet high, made of furry goat's skin dyed red. In his hands he held a flag-staff with a big round banner of colourful bunting.

Then the lama in the tent began to beat the drum, and the old warrior cry 'Kyé, Kyé!'—now a cry for peace—rose into the air. The Sword Dancer began to move: at first he turned in restrained, ceremonial steps, then the round banner began to spin and spread above his head. But, incited by warrior cries and the rolling drum, the dancer rotated faster and faster, so that the banner whirled above him like a parasol. Nevertheless, every step was balanced to demonstrate the cross-wise 'thunderbolt step', symbolically trampling down all evil forces. 'Kyé, Kyé! Victory!' arose the thundering cry, meaning victory for all that is good. Finally, with his sword drawn, its blade shining in the light of the flames, he accompanied his dance with blows and strokes that sliced the night air. All the evil demons were obviously falling to the sword.

It was a fantastic show, with all the symbolic phases of the classical sword dance, the drawing, whetting and lifting of the sword in the traditional way. In the growing darkness the spectators breathlessly swayed to and fro in their places to the rhythm of the dance till the fire had burnt down. The

dancer ended his performance with a last victory cry, thundering through the night, and rolled up his banner. Then all present joined in singing the national anthem.

A New Monster

After the sword dance the fire burnt out and, the last singing voices fading away, everybody went home. The small school children, in their dark blue dresses, were hardly to be seen, because now it was pitch dark. Everywhere during daylight we met these pupils, eager to learn three languages at once and so proud to fulfil their tasks. The most talented of them, passing the primary and secondary school, are chosen for the higher school, such as the college in Tashigang, the easternmost district. It is directed by Father Mackey, who became a true Bhutanese, filled with the wish to guide his pupils, well armed with knowledge, towards modern times. Always anxious to make direct contact with tradition, he even invented a 'magic calendar' to enable his pupils to transfer, in no time, the dates of the old calendar cycle of the zodiac to our modern system.

It happened that a boy of a remote village, who went to school in Mongar before the new road reached that district, was offered the privilege of supplementing his studies in Tashigang. There he went, a jolly mountain boy who had never before seen anything of the technical age. His first essay—he was now seventeen years old—describes his encounter with 'a new monster':

'I was taught at Mongar School for seven years. When in Class VII I was sent to Tashigang. In Mongar I had never seen a motor-car. On my second Sunday in Tashigang, I went to the shop with my friends. We went along a big road, which for me was like a playground. We were playing to-gether, throwing stones and chasing one another, when suddenly I heard a great noise. It was a terrible sound. I looked up and saw a strange monster coming towards me. It had no legs, but it moved. It had two eyes that shone in the sun. From its mouth a kind of smoke was coming. It was crying like a donkey. I was so frightened that I could only stare. It came round a bend in the road. It came close. I ran up the hillside. My friends laughed. They called me back. I stopped, looked down at the strange animal and fell. I rolled down the mountain side to the feet of the animal. I thought I would be eaten or kicked. My friends lifted me up and said "Gari". "What is a Gari?" I asked. They laughed even louder. "A motor-car, a jeep, a one-ton truck!" I stood up and drew close. When the monster stopped a door opened and some men and women got out. I was even more surprised. I looked inside and I thought it was a kind of room, with nice seats inside. I went to the front of the bus. There was a smaller room, with a wheel in the air. In front of the seat was a clock that had a kind of face. I walked around to the front. I put my hand between the two eyes and jumped in surprise because it was very hot. No pony ever had such a hot nose. When the driver saw my face, he told me to get in beside him. He drove a little way. I was more frightened. I had never seen houses and trees move before. Suddenly I thought to myself that I must be moving, though I was not moving my legs. Later I went to Rong-thong in a one-ton truck. This time I was in the back. I was sick. I did not want to return in the truck. I walked back to Tashigang. Now I have driven more often and am used to the motor-car. Now I don't get sick anymore!'

A Democratic King

Young Dorje Wangchu, meeting 'a new monster', is only one of those boys who have had to adapt themselves to the technical age so quickly and who have had to learn how to use its benefits. Since then Dorje has probably learned to drive a car himself. He and his comrades remind us of the small pupils of Cändänbi, who watched the sword dance so intently. The ceremony had been spontaneously arranged in order to pray for the well-being of the King. The whole spectacle was a deep-felt act of devotion to a king who in 1954 had revived the National Assembly, based on the ancient rights of all Bhutias, abandoning his own right of veto. Finally, at the end of 1968, and on the King's own motion, the freely elected National Assembly received full sovereignty, not only to appoint or to reject ministers, but also to force the abdication of any king who might act against the people's interests. By this means the King sought to secure for

57

his democratic monarchy a constitution guaranteeing the future stability of the country. It is no wonder that his people revere him as a saint, and the ringing voices of his villagers sounded very convincing in the Himalayan night:

Long live the King, our noble Lord!
He who protects the lives of all.
He who rules the Dragon State
abounding with sandalwoods.

May all his wisdom still increase,
may all his deeds progress in peace,
may all his power reach the sky,
may all his people multiply!

May all the troubles disappear!
May, in the Kingdom of Bhutan,
Lord Buddha's teachings ever last!
May thus the Sun of Luck appear!

རྒྱལ་པོ་ནི་བརྟན་བཞུགས།

༄༅། སྐྱེ་ཅན་དུ་བཀོད་པའི་རྒྱལ་ཁབ་ན།
ལྔགས་གཉིས་ཀྱི་བསྟན་པ་སྐྱོང་བའི་མགོན།
འབྲུག་རྒྱལ་པོ་མཆན་བདག་རིན་པོ་ཆེ།
སྐུ་འགྱུར་མེད་ཞབས་པད་བརྟན་པར་གསོལ།
ཕྲུགས་དགོངས་པའི་ཤེས་རབ་འཕེལ་འཕེལ་ནས།
ལྔགས་ཚོས་སྤྱིད་ཕྲིན་ལས་གོང་དུ་འཕེལ།
དཔལ་མངའ་ཐང་དགུང་དང་མཉམ་ནས་ཀྱང་།
འབངས་མི་སེར་དར་ཞིང་རྒྱས་པར་གསོལ།
དཔོན་ཚོས་རྗེ་འབྲུག་པའི་རྒྱལ་ཁབ་འདིར།
ཚོས་པ་བས་རྒྱས་བསྟན་པ་རྒྱས་རྒྱས་ནས།
ནད་སྨྱུ་གི་འཁྲུགས་རྩོད་དབྱིངས་སྣ་ཡལ།
བདེ་སྐྱིད་ཀྱི་ཉི་མ་ཤར་བར་གསོག   །།

Illustrations

Bibliographical Notes

BOGLE, George: in C. R. Markham, *Narratives of the Mission of George Bogle to Tibet and of the Journey of Thomas Manning to Lhasa* (London, 1879).

GANSSER, Augusto: *Thron der Götter* (with A. Heim, Zürich, 1938; Eng. trans. *Thrones of the Gods — First Swiss Himalayan Expedition,* London, 1938); *Geology of the Himalayas* (London and New York, 1964); 'Geological Research in the Bhutan Himalaya' (in *The Mountain World,* London, 1966); 'Lunana, the Peaks, Glaciers and Lakes of Northern Bhutan' (in *The Mountain World,* London, 1970).

KUENSEL: 'A fortnightly official Bulletin of the Royal Government of Bhutan' (Thimphu).

OLSCHAK, Blanche C.: *Sikkim — Himalayastaat zwischen Gletschern und Dschungeln* (Zürich, 1965; Eng. trans. *Sikkim — Himalayan State between Glaciers and Jungles,* in preparation); *Perlen alttibetischer Literatur* (Basel, 1967; pocketbook edition *Stufenwege der Erleuchtung,* München, 1970; Eng. trans. *Jewels of Tibetan Literature,* in preparation); *Bhutan — Early History* (a scientific survey with maps, index and a comprehensive bibliography, Tibetan Academy Publications, Zürich und Basel 1971); *Bilder alttibetischer Kunst* (Bern, 1971; Eng. trans. *Pictures of Old-Tibetan Art,* in preparation).

SPENCER CHAPMAN, F.: *Lhasa — the Holy City* (London, 1938).

TURNER, Samuel: *An Account of an Embassy to the Court of the Teshoo Lama in Tibet — Containing the Narrative of a Journey through Bootan and Part of Tibet* (London, 1800).

WHITE, Claude: *Sikhim and Bhutan — Twenty-one Years on the North-Eastern Frontier 1887–1908* (London, 1909).

Contents

1 The rock monastery of Taktshang, the 'Tiger's Den', is built on the sheer face of the cliffs that rise north of Paro in Western Bhutan. Founded at the end of the eighth century, it is still one of the most favoured places of pilgrimage.

aints once meditated
n this small hermitage,
uilt into the perpen-
icular rock wall, below
he 'Tiger's Den', and
nly reachable by
adders.

3
This hermitage, now
eserted, is still visited by
pious pilgrims, praying
and counting their beads.

4
Tsering Kang, bearing the beautiful name 'Glacier of Long Life', guards the northwestern frontier of Bhutan.

5
On the roof of the principal building of the 'Tiger's Den' monks print new prayer flags with the wish, 'Good Fortune and Happiness to all Creatures'.

6
This solitary ruin at the foot of Chomolhari, 'The Sovereign Mistress of the Divine Mountain', was originally built to protect the northwestern frontier.

In the neighbouring mountains prayer flags flutter in the wind above the Mani-shrine of the Dju Gömpa.

8 The strong walls of Paro Dzong shelter the administration and principal monastery of the Paro District.

9 A young novice leans against a door of Paro Dzong. Knocker and mountings are examples of the famous bronze-craft of Bhutan.

10 In Paro Dzong, on New Year's Day, Hero Dances are performed before the gigantic Thanka depicting Guru Rimpoché and his two Mystic Consorts.

11 After the festival the appliqué picture-roll is again carefully rolled up by monks. They put a protective cloth over every image.

12 In the courtyard of the oldest temple of Paro, the Kyichu Lhakhang, are still preserved
   some relics of its earliest foundation, going back to the seventh century.

13 A double rainbow, symbol of the luck-bringing bridge between heaven and earth, appears in the Thimphu Valley above the Chökhor Yangtse Monastery.

14
During a religious
festival in Paro Dzong the
King informally joins his
people.

They watch the tradition
mask dance
The antlered Stag Dance
is just leaping into th
cour

16
The Cemetery Dancers,
with their death-masks,
recall the transience of
life and of all worldly
pleasures.

17
During the 'Dance of the
Big Drums' all evil is
expelled by the sound of
the drums and trampled
into the earth
by 'thunderbolt' steps.

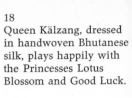

18
Queen Kälzang, dressed in handwoven Bhutanese silk, plays happily with the Princesses Lotus Blossom and Good Luck.

A gay Bhutanese girl plays hide-and-seek when faced with the strange eye of the foreign camera

20 Turquoises, corals and archaic 'eye-stones' form the necklaces of Bhutanese women, who lovingly carry their children on their backs.

21 All Bhutanese people, women included, wear their hair short, the only exception being the women of Laya shown in pictures 50 and 51.

22 The Crown Prince, on a fishing trip, stands on a typical wooden bridge leading to the monastery of Thangthong Gyalpo.

23 The very first visitors to Himalayan regions emphasized the fact that the Bhutanese were among the best-looking people in the mountains.

24 Climbing a rock-stairway leading to a monastery, women carry potatoes and eggs in bamboo baskets to enrich a feast.

25 This boy is displaying consecrated meals of pop-rice and local fruits arranged on bamboo plates.

26
Rocksteps lead to the
'Iron Mountain
Monastery' north of
Thimphu. It was built as
a memorial to the first
resting-place of the
founder of Bhutan,
Zhabdung I, who entered
this region about
A.D. 1600

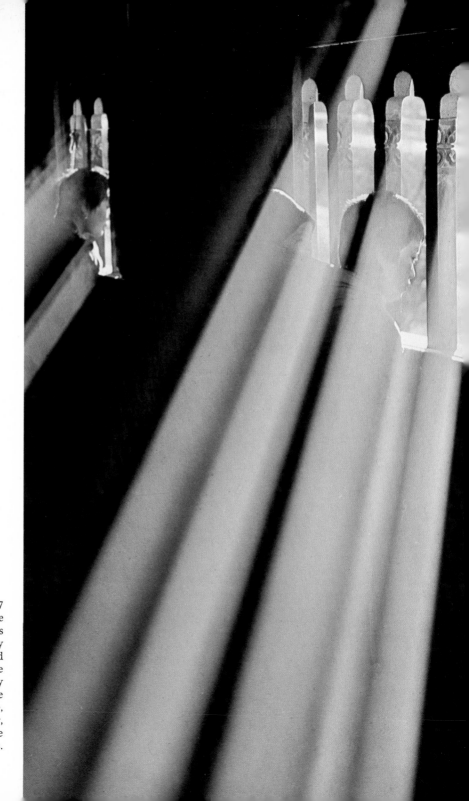

27
Bhutanese houses are
built in the nail-less
frame-work style. They
have glass-less arched
windows which can be
closed from inside by
wooden shutters. The
moke from the wood fire,
glowing in a brazier,
escapes through the
windows.

28 Punakha Dzong, the winter residence of the kings, built at the confluence of 'Father and Mother Rivers'.

29 A swinging suspension bridge walled with plated bamboos. Recently built to an old pattern.

30/31 A holy 'Buddha-tree' grows in front of the temple tower in the main court of
Punakha Dzong, carefully tended by the young monk pupils.

32 Ancient masks hang in front of the screened altar of the protective deities.

33 A praying monk sits before his altar table, flanked by the big standing drum.

34 Simple bamboo suspension bridges over the Mochu to the north of Punakha.
35 Buddhist rock-paintings grace the cliffs overhanging Tsephu Gömpa.

36 A village in a fertile valley on the way to Tongsa Dzong.

37 Ricefields, source of the country's wealth, spread out between highland jungles.

38 The old 'Tiger Fortress' stands above Tongsa Dzong; its round tower is typical of the ancient fortification architecture.

39 Tongsa Dzong, the 'Fortress above the New Village', is the ancestral seat of the royal family of Bhutan and encloses twenty temples within its walls.

40/41 Summoned by the Big Bell, a masterpiece of Bhutanese bronze-casting, monks cross the frame-work galleries to meet in the main court of Tongsa Dzong.

42 To the original western part of Tongsa Dzong were added new buildings and temples;
the latter are distinguished by golden symbols on the roofs above their altars.

43 Shrines are built above rivulets, the water-power from which turns the big prayer-wheels, which symbolically spread blessings in all directions.

44 Skilled in bamboo plaiting, this man makes roofs for granaries, as well as the light bamboo hats which are worn in rain or sun.

45 Maize and bananas are typical of the fertile regions of the country which was known by the Central Asian tribes as 'The Paradise of the South'.

46
In these shrines, built on
the boundaries of temple
districts, twigs from
juniper-trees are burnt to
smoke out all evil powers

The shingle-roofs of Ga
Dzong are covered wi
heavy stones. To the le
in the backgroun
just above the gold
temple symbol, can b
seen the Kang Bu
mountai

48
In the solitude of the
mountain world the
flames of our camp-fire
blaze at the foot of
Chum Kang.

The withered trunk of the
tree emphasises the
loneliness of the mountain
wilderness
the Tarizathang Valley

50/51 The women of Laya, a village situated at 11,400 feet at the foot of the Masa Kang, wear small pointed bamboo hats on their long flowing black hair.

52 The temple tower of the 'Castle of the White Bird', Bjakar Dzong, dominates the whole valley of Bumthang in Eastern Bhutan.

53 The doors of the court of Bjakar Dzong are decorated with colourful symbols.

54 The capitals of the temple pillars are always decorated with beautiful symbols.

55 The most precious relic of Tamshing is the coat of mail of its founder Pämalingpa.

Wearing a crown
scorpion claws ar
covered by a myria
eyes, the lower part
his body being the coil
tail of a snake
the wrathful protector
the planetary cycle
gallops away, surrounded
by flames

58
Old wooden masks are
among the treasures of the
Temple of the Protective
Deities. This bird-head
mask has a third eye and
a crown of skulls.
Being a half mask the
eyes of the wearer peer
out of the gaping mouth.

59
The big standing drums, here decorated with skulls, are beaten with crooked metal drumsticks. During a temple ceremony, they flank the rows of monks, sitting to the left and to the right of the passage leading to the altar in the nave.

60 The 'Monks' Orchestra' of Mongar Dzong, with drums beating and trumpets sounding, strikes up the rhythm for the mask dancers.

61 The antlered Stag Dancer, armed with a sword, demonstrates a surviving form of one of the most ancient traditional magic dances.

62 The dancers with the big drums whirl around, symbolically expelling all evil.

63 The Dancers of Mongar Dzong perform their dramatic rituals until sunset.

e festival to celebrate
e foundation of the
an's Temple, in the
rth of Bumthang, goes
for three days. Leaping
gh through the curtains
the temple door, the
sk dancers take
ssession of the court.

65
The Black Hat Dancer
whirls around till his
silken robes take on the
pearance of a cylinder.
Unchanged by time,
the magic power of the
ritual dances leave a
asting impression on the
beholder.

66 Prayer flags move in the wind above the Mani-stones on the Dong La, the pass connecting the eastern districts of Kürto and Tashiyangtse.

67 Chörten Kora, north of Tashiyangtse, is a great reliquary erected in the style o
Indian stupa, with the eyes of the Mystic Buddha looking in every direction.

The gigantic Himalayan
rhubarb grows up to
an altitude of 12,300 fe
Its stalk, when dried, is
used like an alphorn.

A monk reads in the ear
morning light. In t
background the fortre
of Kurtö emerges from t
mi

70 Prayer flags wave over the Chung La in Western Bhutan. In the background Chomolhari can be seen to the left and Tsering Kang to the right.

71 A yak caravan makes its slow way over the Karakachu La, the western pass leading to Lunana.

72
A big radish is displayed in Lunana, the most remote inhabited valley Bhutan, lying at a heigh of 12,000 feet.

73
Yak breeding is famous
in Lunana, the 'Pass of
the Black Sheep'.
Yak-tails, colourfully dyed,
are the pride of these
mountain people.

74
'Serenity of mind'
is highly esteemed even in
the toughest and coldest
climate. This smiling old
man of Lunana proves it.

75
The women of Lunana
wrap themselves in red
blankets woven from oily
sheep-wool. These
blankets are wind, snow
and rainproof.

small Chörten,
rrounded by prayer
ags, stands on a
ountain-ridge north of
nana. The mountains
cloud form the frontier
Tibet.

77
In this splendid solitude
a lake spreads to the
foot of the gigantic
mountain known as
Kangphu Kang.

78
Chumlhari Kang is one
of the most beautiful
glacier peaks of Lunana.

79
echekanphu Kang is the
wildest mountain on
he Tibetan frontier north
of Lunana.

80 A holy lake of hidden treasures. The jagged walls of snow and ice of the Tsenda Kang mountain chain are mirrored on its frozen surface.